PRESIDENTIAL
SEARCH

By John W. Nason
Assisted By Nancy R. Axelrod

Contents

Foreword

The Association of Governing Boards has long been concerned with the presidential selection process. The choice of a new president or chancellor is the most important and far-reaching responsibility of any board, and it has remained a frequent subject of inquiry to AGB staff for several years.

Recognizing the importance of the quality of the selection process to the entire higher education enterprise, the W. K. Kellogg Foundation generously funded our proposal to develop a set of guidelines for search and selection committees. We express our thanks to the Foundation, and to Dr. Arlon Elser who served as our program officer, for their understanding of the significance of this study and for their support in making it possible.

The simplest part of this project was selecting the individual most qualified to serve as project director: Dr. John W. Nason brought to this task a distinguished record of service as president of Carleton and Swarthmore colleges and trustee of Vassar College. This monograph is an in-depth examination of one of the thirteen board responsibilities he addresses in *The Nature of Trusteeship: The Role and Responsibility of College and University Governing Boards.* We are grateful to him for accepting yet another assignment which demanded his special talents.

Nancy R. Axelrod, Vice President for Programs and Public Policy at AGB, was selected to work as Assistant Director to John Nason because of her past work with board members who sought guidance in presidential search and other governance matters. We take pride in her many contributions to the effort.

This project has been enriched by the guidance of the knowledgeable and experienced members who served as the Advisory Board for this project. Their individual and highly diverse institutional perspectives were a constant reminder to the project staff that there is no single or completely fail-safe way to conduct a presidential search. The members of the Advisory Board are listed following this foreword.

The presidents, trustees, and other educators who served on this board directed John Nason to address the procedures of presidential search in one single document. While emphasizing the similarities in presidential search, selection, and appointment across institutional lines, the text does point out some of the differences that must be take into consideration for public and private, two-year, four-year, and multicampus institutions. The text also attempts to provide boards and search committees with choices that must be considered on the basis of the many subtle but important factors which enter the picture.

The presidential selection process should be viewed as an opportunity to establish a foundation upon which a review of presidential performance may subsequently be conducted by the board. Clearly defined criteria of performance and a statement of board expectations presented to the president at the time of his or her appointment should be an essential part of the presidential assessment process.

This report is a companion volume to *Presidential Assessment: A Guide to the Periodic Review of the Performance of Chief Executives,* which compliments AGB's earlier development of procedural guidelines and criteria for self-study by boards of trustees.* We believe that when a board wisely chooses to assess its organization and performance, it is also reviewing the performance of the chief executive. Likewise, a board that joins with its chief executive to review the effectiveness of the office of the president is also looking at is own viability as an organization.

Robert L. Gale
President
August 1984

---

* *Self-Study Guidelines and Criteria* are available for Community College Governing Boards, Private College and University Governing Boards, Public College and University Governing Boards, Governing Boards of Public Higher Education Systems, and Boards of State Postsecondary Education Planning and Coordinating Agencies.

Advisory Board Members *

*Since this study was completed the affiliations of some of the Advisory Board have changed.

Preface
to Revised Edition

T he latest available figures indicate that the average tenure of American college and university presidents is 6½ years. Some, unhappily, last only one year; others seem to continue indefinitely.[1] Approximately 500 colleges and universities are looking for new presidents each year.

With such a substantial number of new presidents being selected each year, one would think that fairly standard procedures would have been established and that boards of trustees would know from experience and example how best to proceed. A variety of effective procedures have indeed emerged, but unhappy mistakes continue to be made—mistakes that are costly to the institution and that could have been avoided with better governing board understanding and search committee performance. This document is a practical guide to the process of selecting and appointing new presidents.

The original study was made in 1978 under a grant from the W.K. Kellogg Foundation. Questionnaires were sent to the board chairperson, the chairperson of the selection committee (who might be the same person), and the president of each of the 450 colleges and universities that we could readily identify as having appointed new presidents in 1975-76 and 1976-77. Replies were received from 326 institutions or 72%.

Recognizing that the full story of the successes and failures of the selection process is rarely made public, we selected 22 institutions of various types—public and private, four-year and two-year, predominantly black, women's, church-related—for personal investigation. So far as possible, the president and all members of the search and selection committee or committees were individually interviewed. These conversations provided an extraordinarily candid composite picture of how the president was selected and, at times, a startling impression of the different viewpoints and interpretations of individual members.

The first version was published in 1979. Much attention has been given to the problem during the past five years, and this new edition attempts to distill and codify some of the practical wisdom that has been emerging.

The original study was guided and shaped by the members of a distinguished advisory board. It was enriched by the wisdom and experience of Joseph F. Kauffman, Professor of Educational Administration at the University of Wisconsin-Madison and author of two of the best books on college and university presidents, who served as consultant.

This revised edition has profited greatly from the many suggestions that President Merle F. Allshouse of Bloomfield College collected from users of the first edition; the perceptive comments of Frederic W. Ness and Ronald S. Stead, experts in the field, have also been enormously useful.

I am indebted in this undertaking as in others to the constant encouragement and help of Bob Gale and Tom Ingram, President and Executive Vice President respectively of the Association of Governing Boards, and I have a special indebtedness to AGB Vice President Nancy Axelrod who served as assistant director of the study, dug up much of the material, processed the questionnaires, and helped with the field work. She deserves to be billed as co-producer. This revised edition would not have been possible without the assistance of Linda Henderson who was indefatigable in corralling reluctant statistics and elusive sources of information.

John W. Nason
Keene, N. Y.
April 1984

---

1. The Preliminary 1983/1984 Compensation and Benefits Survey of College and University Chief Executive Officers, prepared under the aegis of the Association of Governing Boards of Universities and Colleges and the College and University Personnel Association, April 1984, reports that 18% of presidents have held their present offices for one year or less and 20% for 11 years or more.

Introduction

Some Preliminary Cautions

I t is commonly asserted that the most important single responsibility of a board of trustees is the selection and appointment of a new president.[1] This responsibility is important because the president occupies the central role in the life of the institution. As the agent of the board and the embodiment of its authority, the president is the most powerful and influential individual in the academic community. Externally the president is seen not only as representing the institution and its values but also as determining those values and therefore the institution's contribution to society. Internally the president is looked to for educational leadership and is expected to direct and control what in a large university can be a complex and difficult academic orchestra.[2]

The selection of the right person to be president is crucial for the life and health of the institution. Success depends on careful planning, well thought out procedures, a very considerable amount of work, and the constant attention of those board members assigned to the task. This is so obvious that one is constantly surprised by the careless and often shoddy way in which many boards go about the business. Certain general considerations illuminate the complexities of the job and serve as cautions against hasty or ill-considered action.

1. Changing role of the president. The kaleidoscopic character of postsecondary education since World War II requires people of very different talents for different types of institution and, indeed, for the same institution at different stages in its life. The traditional image of the benign scholar-administrator is as archaic as the institution over which he or she presided. The extraordinary growth of higher education since the end of World War II, the proliferation of subject matter and services to satisfy the demands of new clienteles, the advent of collective bargaining, the increasing involvement of state and federal agencies, the turbulence of the 1960s, and now the financial pressures resulting from declining enrollments and the prospect of declining resources—these and many other factors have complicated the presidential task.

Should we look for scholars to lead the faculty, managers to coordinate complex operations, fund raisers *par excellence*, negotiators to arbitrate and compromise conflicting forces and constituencies, educational statesmen with vision and charisma? There is no longer a single model of the model college president. *Before deciding whom they want, boards must decide what they want.* They must decide where the institution is, where it is going or should go in the next five to ten years, and what kind of person can best lead it there.[3]

2. *Shared governance*. One of the major complicating factors in college and university administration has been the diffusion of presidential power through what has come to be called shared governance. Colleges and universities are not political democracies, though there are some people who would have them so organized. Never-

theless, the principle that government should rest on the consent of the governed is today so widely held in the academic world that participation by faculty and increasingly by students and alumni in the selection of a new president is often considered necessary for the legitimation of his or her authority. In many state universities such participation is mandated by law. And where the governor is not a member of the board *ex officio*, it is not uncommon to consult the governor, as well as other state officials and influential legislators.

3. *Growth of systems*. The last quarter century has seen the rise of educational systems that may include several campuses or institutions as in Illinois, statewide networks by types of institution as in California, or all postsecondary educational institutions as in New York. In some states colleges and universities within a system have their own boards, which have a major voice in the selection of the president. In most, however, there is a single system board governing all educational units within the system. Presidents are appointed by the system board, usually on the recommendation of the chief officer of the system. The process of selection will often differ from that followed by the board of a single college or university. It may require more levels of approval, and its steps will often be mandated by the bylaws of the system.

4. *Equal opportunity requirements*. The mid-60s saw the beginning of federal and state legislation respecting equal opportunity employment and affirmative action. Employment, promotion, and compensation (in education as well as elsewhere) are now subject to a slightly bewildering series of federal and state laws and bureaucratic regulations. The impact of these regulations varies with the type of institution and with the extent and nature of government contracts. Thus, public universities in general and independent universities with large government contracts for research must comply with strict requirements for publicizing vacancies, must refrain from seeking information about a candidate's race, color, religion, and marital status, must ensure equal opportunity for all applicants, and in some cases must take affirmative action in employing women and minorities. Independent colleges and universities without extensive contracts are not under the same constraints, although they too are obligated by Title VII and state laws to practice non-discrimination in all personnel matters. Many small colleges that have announced that they are EO/AA employers have preferred to lean over backwards in following the spirit of the law.

5. Academic preference for outsiders. The preference of the academic world for selecting outside candidates rather than following the common business practice of training a successor from within presents a further complication. Recent studies indicate that approximately 30% of college and university presidents are promoted from within. This is the reverse of what happens in the business world.

One reason is to be found in the nonhierarchical nature of educational institutions. Faculty members have a substantial role in governance, as previously noted. Presidents have diminished authority, and attempts to train their successors tend to be viewed with suspicion, if not hostility.

Furthermore, as we shall see in Chapter III, institutional needs are apt to change over the course of time. The selection of a new president provides an opportunity to bring in a person with different qualities and strengths from those of his or her predecessor. For this reason it is generally considered wise for the outgoing president not to participate in the final choice of successor (although participation in the search phases may be helpful).

Finally, the selection of a member of the faculty or current administration presents political problems. Unless some one individual stands head and shoulders above the rest and commands respect from a wide spectrum of the faculty, the choice of a member of one department or school is likely to be seen as precursor to a probable shift in institutional values and programs. The prospect creates apprehension. Furthermore, administrative officers suffer the disadvantage of inevitably having made decisions unpopular in certain quarters. Somehow their defects loom larger than their virtues, and internal constituencies tend to prefer the uncertain qualities of the outsider to the known weaknesses or alleged biases of the insider.

A change in the leadership of a college or university is in most cases a profoundly disturbing event, for it involves, or should involve, a reappraisal of the values and direction of the institution. An insider would seem to have the obvious advantage of knowing the institution and being able to keep it on course; and in times of emergency faculty members as well as trustees are likely to turn to such a person. The time may come when this procedure is more widely followed. At present, however, the outsider is generally perceived by the faculty and administrative staff to be less threatening to their particular interests and so gets the initial support that is so essential to future success.[4]

6. *Crisis versus normal transition*. The problem boards face when a vacancy occurs in the office of the president vary with the nature of the president's departure. A considerable number of these vacancies are the result of normal retirement or resignation for a variety of personal and professional reasons. In these situations ample advance notice of the transition has normally been given, so that plans can be carefully made for the choice of a successor. Other causes of vacancies are serious illness or death in office, sudden resignations in the face of personal or institutional catastrophe, and resignations under pressure. There is clearly a difference between the transition that has been foreseen well in advance and the crisis situation that catches the institution and its board of trustees unaware and unprepared.

The frequency of unanticipated departures should provide a cautionary note to boards of trustees: it is well to have one's machinery and procedures in place well before the event. The situation at the University of Vermont provides a good example of the problem. When, in 1974, the president suddenly announced his resignation (to accept a new post in this case), the university was facing a series of crises—a comprehensive planning program, the challenge of collective bargaining, pressure to reduce expenditures. "The resignation could not have come at a more inopportune time," writes John W. Moore, Associate Vice President. "At that point we learned an important lesson: A university should maintain a fully developed procedure for handling the resignation of the president and for organizing the search for a new chief executive."[5]

7. *No single correct method*. The best procedure of search and selection for one college may not be best for another. The large state university surrounded by diverse political pressures may need to establish safeguards that would be unnecessary for a small church-related college. Institutions operating under sunshine laws must proceed differently from those which do not. A college that has run through three presidents in five years has a different problem on its hands from one that is seeking a successor to a president who is retiring after 25 successful years. All search and selection efforts should include in some fashion the steps described in the following chapters; but the manner in which they take each step and the relative importance accorded each will vary from one institution to the next. One important key to success is *flexibility*.

8. *Myth of the perfect president*. There is no such thing as the ideal college or university president. The differing needs of different institutions and the complex demands made on the president require different people with often quite different skills and qualities. No one possesses them all. The man or woman who might be a brilliant success at one institution may be a dismal failure at another. The important thing is the fit between the individual and the institution. Some candidates will clearly fit better than others, but an adequate search process should discover more than one individual who would be "ideal" for the institution involved. People change. Some grow under the pressures and opportunities of the position. The individual who looks less than perfect at the start may prove in time to be a winner.

Additional Sources of Information

Joseph F. Kauffman: *The Selection of College and University Presidents*, Association of American Colleges 1974. This is the best brief analysis and set of guidelines on the topic—well worth the time of trustees and members of search and selection committees.

Frederick deW. Bolman: *How College Presidents Are Chosen*, American Council on Education 1965. An older but highly readable treatment based on a survey of 116 private and public colleges and universities.

Warren Bennis: *The Leaning Ivory Tower*, Jossey-Bass Publishers 1973. An entertaining account of the author's experience in various administrative posts and as a candidate before a dozen selection committees "being examined rather like a bolt of felt, as I sometimes thought."

There is an extensive literature on the changing nature of the president's job and of the current expectations faced by presidents. A few of the more perceptive and useful treatments are:

Joseph F. Kauffman: *At the Pleasure of the Board*, American Council on Education 1980. A perceptive treatment of the president's role and problems.

Clark Kerr: *Presidents Make a Difference: Strengthening Leadership in Colleges and Universities,* Association of Governing Boards 1984. The report of AGB's Commission on Strengthening Presidential Leadership.

Robert F. Carbone: *Presidential Passages*, American Council on Education 1981. Short, pithy, disturbing.

Frederic W. Ness: *An Uncertain Glory*, Jossey-Bass Publishers 1971. An entertaining and illuminating series of vignettes of presidential life by an old hand.

James L. Fisher: *Power of the Presidency*, Macmillan Publishing Company 1984. Reflections on the use of presidential power designed primarily for the benefit of presidents, but useful for those seeking presidents.

Michael D. Cohen and James G. March: *Leadership and Ambiguity: The American College President*, a report prepared for the Carnegie Commission on Higher Education, McGraw-Hill 1974. Provocative and controversial.

Lewis B. Mayhew and James R. Glenn, Jr.: "College and University Presidents: Roles in Transition" in *Liberal Education*, vol. 61, no. 3, Oct. 1975. A useful survey of the changing roles in the 19th and 20th centuries.

John D. Millet: "The Multiple Roles of the College and University President," American Council on Education 1976.

1. Clark Kerr, former president of the University of California and chairman of the former Carnegie Commission on Higher Education, contends that selection is the second most important responsibility, the first being the creation of a presidential office that is viable and attractive. See chapter I of *Presidents Make A Difference: Strengthening Leadership in Colleges and Universities*, a report of the National Commission on Strengthening Presidential Leadership, published by the Association of Governing Boards, 1984. This report should be read in its entirety by every search and selection committee.

2. "With all his travel, however, all his limitations of time and insight," wrote Douglas Knight 25 years ago when president of what is now Lawrence University, "he is the one person who gives his allegiance to the whole institution. He is committed to the *relationship* of all the varied enterprises that make up his community, and no other person in that community has them all equally at heart." *Association of American Colleges Bulletin*, vol. 44, no. 4, December 1958, p. 646. The article carries the title, "The Waking Nightmare: Or How Did I Get Into This?"

3. See bibliography at the end of the chapter for a few references to the extensive literature on the changing nature of the president's job.

4. One of the most interesting treatments of this problem is to be found in Robert Birnbaum's "Presidential Succession: An Institutional Analysis," *Educational Record*, vol. 52, no. 2, Spring 1971. For a somewhat different view *see* Paul C. Reinert's article in *AGB Reports*, vol. 16, no. 7, April 1974.

5. "Candor and Communication Mark Presidential Search," *CASE Currents*, vol. 2, no. 9, October 1976, p. 10.

Chapter 1

Step One—
Establishing the Machinery
of Search and Selection

henever a vacancy occurs in the presidency of a college or university, the board of trustees must either create or activate one or more committees to search out suitable candidates, to screen them, and to recommend one or more for final action by the board. Among state institutions bylaws frequently specify the composition of the committee(s) and the procedure to be followed. Here and there farsighted boards of trustees of independent colleges have adopted resolutions well in advance defining the steps to be taken. In both situations, however, individuals must be chosen to serve and the machinery set in motion. Unfortunately most boards tend to postpone decisions about the search and selection process until the last moment, sometimes with disastrous results. It would be wise for every board to establish in advance the framework for the selection of the next president.

Acting or Interim Presidents:
Pro and Con

When presidents retire or announce their resignation well in advance, there is time for the machinery of search and selection to function in a satisfactory fashion. When, however, the president dies, becomes too ill to serve, or leaves under pressure and on short notice, the board faces an emergency. Should it engage in a crash program to find a new president, or should it appoint an acting or interim president?

"It is my considered opinion," writes

Frederic W. Ness, then President of the Association of American Colleges, "that many colleges and universities, when confronted with a presidential change, are in fact *not* ready for a new leadership and that by a premature selection they do the institution disservice that can seriously affect its future."[1] The obvious advantages of naming an acting president, as Ness proceeds to point out, are (1) time for the kind of institutional study of goals and needs on which a presidential search could be intelligently based and (2) help from the acting president who can "guide the trustees through the intricacies of the search and selection process." An acting president may be found within or without the institution. Other things being equal, it is desirable that the interim president not be a candidate for the permanent position, especially if he or she is already a member of the faculty or staff; but there are instances where the interim president has become permanent.

On the other hand, the appointment of an acting president is a holding operation. Outgoing presidents, unless their departure is sudden and unexpected, tend not to promote major changes in their last year in office. Incoming presidents usually wait at least a year before advocating new policies of a major nature. With an acting president for a year in between, the institution experiences a three-year period of indecisive leadership—indecisive in the sense that major changes in or reaffirmations of policy and of program are largely postponed. Trustees, faculty, and students who have lived through such periods know how frustrating they can be.

When faced with a crisis precipitated by the death or sudden departure of the president, trustees have little option but to appoint an acting president. The question is whether more boards would be wise to follow Ness's advice. Cohen and March, in their study of current college presidents, estimate that since World War II, about 4 percent of college and university presidents have held strictly temporary appointments.[2] It may well be that more institutions should follow this practice which, as pointed out, has the advantage of giving boards time to determine the needs of their institution and consequently the qualities most appropriate for the new president before setting up the machinery of search and selection.

What Kind of Committee(s)?

Unless the machinery of search and selection has already been determined, trustees or regents have four options.[3]

1. To constitute themselves a committee of the whole or to create a special board committee.

2. To appoint a single search and selection committee with representatives from various constituencies.

3. To establish two committees—one search and one screening.

4. To appoint a trustee committee plus one or more advisory committees of faculty, students, and others.

1. Community college boards, which tend to be relatively small, often prefer to keep control of the entire process in their own hands. As the chairman of one community college reported: "Since, by law, it is the

responsibility of the board to appoint the president this duty was not shared or delegated." In those church-related colleges or universities where it is stipulated that the president must be a member of the religious order or denomination, the number of available candidates is often so small and the individuals so well known that the board can proceed without setting up committees of search and selection. Very occasionally an internal candidate is so obvious a choice that the board makes the appointment, preferably in consultation with the faculty, without undertaking a search. These are special situations. In most instances the exclusion of faculty and other constituencies would be counterproductive.

2. The most common practice is the single search and selection committee. Normally such a committee is composed of trustees, faculty, students and not infrequently alumni, administrative officers, line staff, representatives of the community. Critics of the single committee complain that it is too large to be efficient and that, by being representative of all or at least several constituencies and trading off their various preferences, it runs the risk of ending up with mediocre candidates. "In my view," wrote a member of the selection committee of a liberal arts college, "the broad-based search committee is most likely (on the average campus) to produce a compromise candidate. In many instances this may not be the best result for the institution—a quantum jump may be needed."

On the other hand, the response to our survey was replete with comments about the unifying effect of joint committees. Typical

of these was the statement by the search committee chairperson of a state university: "Our process worked so well that the individual constituencies became a committee of the whole and disregarded their particular loyalties. As a result, nothing would deter them from seeking the most highly qualified candidate for the presidency. . . . Truly a unique committee with a singular mission."

3. A less common method is the establishment of two committees — one for search and the other for screening, or one for search and screening and the second for selection of the final acceptable candidates. Frequently, the former consists of faculty, students, and others, with one or two trustees as liaison (though some have no trustees), while the latter is composed of trustees. This arrangement has the advantage of dividing up the work and in particular of assigning the most time-consuming stages, the search and preliminary screening, to faculty or to faculty, students, and staff who have the interest and can afford the time necessary. It further reassures local groups—faculty in particular, but also, in community colleges, local sponsors and influential citizens—that the new president will be acceptable to them, because those not acceptable will have been screened out.

The danger in the dual committee system lies in the opportunity for the search and screening committee (composed of nontrustees or dominated by faculty with only one or two trustees as members) to usurp the function of the selection committee. It can dictate the final choice by concluding that only one candidate is suitable or by giving one individual so strong a priority rating as to amount to the same thing. The chairman of a distinguished private university, for example, reported: "The search was originated on the theory that there would be a search committee to screen candidates and recommend five to six qualified candidates to the selection committee. . . . However, the search committee and particularly the faculty and students thereof began to regard themselves as the selection committee." He goes on to suggest that the next time he would recommend a single selection committee with advisory committees of faculty, students, and administrators.

4. This brings us to the fourth option—a search and selection committee composed of trustees (or nearly so) buttressed by a series of advisory committees representing faculty, students, alumni, and occasionally others. This permits consultation with faculty, students, and other constituencies while keeping the selection process in the hands of those primarily responsible for the final appointment. It helps to avoid the polarization between trustees and these other groups to which reference has already been made. It keeps the central committee of selection small enough to be manageable—a frequent criticism that surfaced in our survey being the unwieldly size of committees.[4] On the other hand, the problem of communication creates irritation. Committees are not always sure of their function. Faculty and students often resent what they consider to be second-class membership.

Many public colleges and universities have bylaw provisions or formal board resolutions specifying how committees will be constituted. They vary from the very simple to the quite complex. The regulations of a Texas university simply state: "In case a change in the presidency is made, the board will accept for consideration suggested nominations from a screening committee representing the Board, the faculty, and the student body, which committee shall be appointed by the Board."

An eastern state university prescribes a search committee of three trustees, three faculty, three alumni and two students, with the duty of screening applicants and recommending a predetermined number to the board's nominating committee. The nominating committee in turn selects two or three individuals from the list submitted to recommend to the board, which then makes the appointment.

In a statewide system such as the California State University and Colleges procedures are quite complex. The board chairperson appoints a 13-member Presidential Selection Advisory Committee that conducts an elaborate search under clearly outlined conditions that leave most of the action in the chancellor's office. The five trustee members of the committee are the only voting members. With advice from the other members and with help from the chancellor's office the candidates are reduced to three or four who are presented to the board for selection and appointment.

The choice of committee structure will vary with the institution and should be made with individual circumstances in mind. Here and elsewhere, flexibility should be a guiding principle. The temper of the campus and the degree of trust among trustees, administration, faculty, and students will influence the choice. Where relations are reasonably harmonious, structure is less important. Where relations are strained, the committee structure does become important and should be given careful thought. The single committee composed of representatives of several constituencies is the most common mode. It avoids the difficulties of communication and logistics that often plague multiple committees. Its outstanding advantage, however, is the strong sense of unity and common enterprise that the joint work of the committee generates. Respondent after respondent testified to the new perspectives and broader understanding that resulted from trustees, faculty, and students working together for a common goal. This is a fringe benefit not to be minimized.

Size of Committee

The size of search or search and selection committees will vary according to the pattern outlined in the previous section. Single committees tend to be larger; multiple committees, smaller. The range in our survey was as follows:

	range	median
4-year public	3-21	10
2-year public	3-17	11
private university	6-21	10
4-year private college	4-25	10
4-year church-related	3-21	10
2-year private	7-17	10

The uniformity in both the range and median figures is striking. The size at the upper end of the range explains the frequency of the criticism that committees were too large to be efficient—both with respect to regularity of attendance and to meeting the deadline for recommendations. On the other hand, the value of a committee representing various constituencies must not be minimized. The trade-off between size and representation will have to be made by each board. Experience suggests that a committee of nine or ten works best.[5]

Composition of Committee

Most single search and selection committees represent different groups. While there is a danger, as we have noted, that diverse viewpoints will cancel each other out, eliminating the strongest candidates, diversity can provide an important plus factor in assessing qualifications. The participation of faculty, students, alumni, state education officials, and local citizens in the selection process legitimates, as it were, the final choice.

There are still trustees who look upon faculty as employees with no proper voice in either policy decisions or presidential appointments, as there are still faculty who view trustees as interlopers who know nothing about education and should not be involved in so important an exercie as selecting a president. Fortunately, these types are becoming less numerous. Most boards now recognize the legitimate concern of faculty in the selection process. "Joint effort" is specifically recommended in the formal *Statement on Government of Colleges and Universities*, adopted in 1966 by the American Association of University Professors and recommended by the American Council on Education and the Association of

	trustees only	faculty	students	alumni[7]	no trustees
4-year public	9%	92%	92%	66%	22%
2-year public	12	82	88	35	24
private university	7	67	67	60	} 36
4-year private college	25	68	61	54	
4-year church-related	11	67	62	49	32
2-year private	13	88	38	63	0

Governing Boards to their respective members as a "significant step forward in the clarification of the respective roles of governing boards, faculties and administration."[6]

It should be kept in mind that the board is in the last analysis responsible for the search process and therefore decides who shall or shall not serve. Faculty, student, and other participation is by invitation, not by right. A board may be unwise not to include faculty and others, but it has no legal obligation to do so unless bylaws or state regulations dictate membership.

The following table shows the percent of participation of trustees, faculty, students, and alumni on selection committees, as reported in our survey. It does not indicate the extent of membership in publicly supported institutions of local citizens, state education officials, or other politicians.

Selecting Committee Members

A good committee will be one with a high degree of mutual respect and trust among its members. This may not exist at first, but with the right selection of members and with the leadership of the chairperson, it should emerge as the result of working for a common concern.

What qualities should one seek in committee members? So far as possible— commitment to the institution, an understanding of its programs and problems, breadth of experience, a capacity for balanced judgment, discretion, and the ability to recognize the validity and to respect the integrity of viewpoints differing from one's own. Ideally, the committee should reflect the diversity of the institution by including one or more women and one or more members of minority groups.[8]

This is a large order, and the question can properly be asked, how does one arrive at a committee composed of such people? If we exclude the one instance in our survey where all members of the committee were appointed by the outgoing president, four methods of selecting committee members have been followed.

1. In some instances the board or the executive committee of the board or its chairman make all appointments. Presumably some advice is given or suggestions made regarding the nontrustee members. This method has the advantage of making reasonably sure that difficult or disruptive members will not serve. It is likely to anger both faculty and students by denying them

the privilege of making their own choices.

2. The most common practice is for each group to select its own members to serve on the committee. Sometimes board or faculty will seek to control the selection of students, but in general, faculty choose faculty members and students the student members. The alumni association may ask one or more of the officers of the association (already elected by the alumni) to serve *ex officio*. This gives the various constituencies the greatest sense of participation; and if there is full agreement on the person chosen, the new president starts his or her career with a high degree of acceptance. On the other hand, there is no certainty that the committee will be truly representative of diverse interests within the institution or that the resulting mixture will be harmonious and effective.

3. One way of reducing the disadvantages of allowing each group to designate its own members is to have the board lay down certain general criteria for selecting committee members. It may specify, for example, that one faculty member should be chosen by each division of the university or that there should be an equal number of senior and junior members of the faculty; that one student should come from a graduate or professional school and the other from the undergraduate college, or that one student should be male and the other female.

4. A second way is to invite various constituencies to nominate several candidates for committee membership with the understanding that the board or the chairperson will appoint committee members from among those so nominated.

This allows the board a certain latitude in setting up the committee while recognizing the legitimate concern of faculty, students, and others to have a real voice in the matter.

In large complex universities it is probably desirable, if not in fact essential, that the nature of each committee member and the method of selection or appointment be spelled out in detail, as suggested in method number 3 above. In smaller and less complex institutions method number 2 usually works fairly well if there is a considerable degree of harmony and trust among the various groups. Where this does not exist, method number 4 may reduce some of the friction of antagonistic positions.

It is not uncommon for the chairperson of the board to serve on the committee. "It is very important," commented one respondent, "that the chairman of the board of trustees serve on the presidential search committee. The chairman of the board works more closely with the president than does any other member of the board of trustees. Consequently, the relationship between the chairman of the board and the president should be good." Not everyone agrees, however, that the board chairperson should serve on the committee. It is suggested that the chairperson, being a strong and often powerful personality, may dominate the committee. There have been instances where the chairperson pushed for his or her favorite candidate over the opposition of the committee, usually with unfortunate results.

A less controversial point is the appointment of the affirmative action officer to the committee, which has been done in a number of cases. The affirmative action officer should certainly be consulted to make sure that no mistakes are made, but there is no need for his or her constant presence, which can in certain circumstances be intimidating as well as casting doubt on the fair-mindedness of the committee members.

There are obvious advantages in having a seasoned and trusted administrative officer on the committee. He or she will know better than most the nature of the president's job and will be able to assess candidates in the light of that knowledge. On the other hand, such an officer may be too close to the president's office for comfort; his or her opinions may carry more weight than they deserve.

In addition, it is questionable whether an officer who will report directly to the new president should participate in his or her selection.

The Charge to the Committee

The final phase of Step One is a clear statement of the committee's mandate. The board should make sure everyone interested in the selection of the new president knows the composition of the committee and the extent of its authority. Many a committee has run into difficulty due to ambiguity on the latter. Some boards will prefer to leave details of procedure largely to the committee; others will want to provide quite specific instructions. Items that might be included in the charge are the following:

1. Development of institutional needs and consequent criteria for selecting the new president, or statement of criteria to be followed if the board has already developed a needs statement.

2. Membership on the committee(s) including any instructions regarding the methods of selection and the choice of chairperson.

3. Timetable providing dates by which the board expects recommendations from the committee.

4. Breadth of search for candidates. Some boards have instructed their committees on where to look; others leave this to the committees themselves.

5. Necessity of complying with equal opportunity/affirmative action requirements. Some boards have even specified methods of screening candidates.

6. Availability of funds for committee expenses.

7. Desirability of using outside professional consultants.

8. Degree of confidentiality or openness (e.g., sunshine laws) expected of committee.

9. Number of candidates to be recommended to the board for final decision and whether these candidates are to be ranked or not.

10. Unambiguous statement of the board's intention to make the final choice and appointment.

By no means do all of the above need to be included in a formal charge to the committee, but some obviously should be. To clear the air regarding the committee's responsibilities and authority, the committee's mandate should be made public.

Several of the items mentioned above will be examined in detail in the following chapter.

Checklist #1
Establishing the Machinery

1. Is the institution ready for a presidential search or should an acting or interim president be appointed?

2. Who will conduct the search and selection processes?

  a. Board as a whole or a committee of the board.

  b. Single search and selection committee composed of trustees, faculty, students, and others.

  c. Dual committee structure—search committee in which non-trustees predominate, selection committee in which trustees prdominate.

  d. Single trustee search and selection committee aided by one or more *advisory* committees of faculty, students, etc.

3. What size of committee?

4. How will committee members be appointed?

  a. By the board, its executive committee, or the chairperson.

  b. Each group elects its own members.

  c. Each group elects under restrictions set by board.

  d. Board or chairperson selects from nominations presented by each group.

5. Does the machinery of selection reflect the diversity of the institutional community? Is its final recommendation likely to get widespread campus support?

6. Has the board made clear to the committee(s) *in writing*—and to the public—the extent of and the limits to the committee's authority?

In many public institutions, especially those that are part of statewide systems, the answers to some of these questions are mandated by law or bureaucratic regulation. Even where the chief executive officer of the system or the state's board of regents has the final choice, however, local institutional boards tend to exercise much more authority when it is a question of selecting a new president—and they should make most of it.

1. "The Right Time: The Wrong Question" in *AGB Reports*, vol. 13, no. 9, July/August 1971, p. 6.

2. *Leadership and Ambiguity: The American College President*, McGraw-Hill 1974, pp. 165-166.

3. The terms used to describe committee functions can be confusing. Search committees are sometimes limited to generating a roster of candidates, as discussed in Chapter 4, and sometimes are expected to carry the process through to the recommendation of one or more acceptable candidates to the board of trustees. Similarly, selection committees rarely "select" the new president; they screen the candidates and nominate or recommend one or more to the board for appointment. Some institutions use the term "screening committee" for this function.

4. Various commentators on the selection process recommend this formula. See Joseph F. Kauffman: *The Selection of College and University Presidents*, pp. 27-28; Manning M. Pattillo: "How to Choose a College President" in *AGB Reports*, vol. 15, no. 5, February 1973; Paul C. Reinert: "The Problem with Search Committees" in *AGB Reports*, vol. 16, no. 7, April 1974.

5. In a study of 52 selected universities (both doctoral degree granting and comprehensive) and liberal arts colleges that had undertaken presidential searches in 1980-81, Judith B. McLaughlin, Research Associate at Harvard's Graduate School of Education, found that among the private institutions 24 set up search committees ranging from 5 to 12 members and 4 institutions had committees ranging from 13 to 16 members, whereas only 4 public institutions established committees from 9 to 12 members and 19 of these public institutions had committees with from 15 to 30 members. Unpublished doctoral thesis, Harvard Graduate School of Education, 1983.

6. "If controlling bodies," writes Warren Bennis, former President of the University of Cincinnati, "insist upon dictating university presidents, instead of selecting men by more democratic processes, the campus must expect resistance from all those excluded from the selection process. The president forced on a reluctant university accepts a job that is difficult in the best of times. If students or faculty perceive his appointment as coercive, his job becomes impossible. In these uncertain times, no president has time to spend winning over sulky constituents. I am convinced that no university president, hard-line, soft-line, whatever his style, can overcome the handicap of a peremptory appointment. A selection process that is not broadly representative hamstrings the man it settles on. Moreover, the process itself may become an explosive issue, as it did for Pitzer at Stanford." *The Leaning Ivory Tower*, Jossey-Bass Publishers 1973, p. 65.

7. The percentage for alumni unreliable because some respondents apparently counted alumni faculty and trustees as alumni, while others included alumni only when appointed as a result of their status as alumni.

8. See Edward Kern: "Quest for a Silver Unicorn" in *Life*, vol. 70, no. 21, June 4, 1971, for a vivid example of what can happen with disruptive committee members.

Chapter 2

Step Two— Organizing the Committee

O nce the presidential search committee has been formed and its charge from the board received, the committee must plan its campaign. Various practical arrangements are essential, and certain agreements on procedure need to be nailed down at the start.[1]

The Committee Chairperson

The chairperson is the most important member of the committee. He or she sets the tone of the committee, directs the discussion, smooths ruffled feelings, copes with emergencies. In public institutions, it is the chairperson who diverts political pressures and demonstrates by his or her impartiality the nonpartisan nature of the search. On the outside, the chairperson is official spokesman, interpreter of the committee's work to the public, and in most situations the liaison between the institution and the candidates. He or she must command respect, must be impartial, discreet, incisive, and humane. In addition, the chairperson usually serves as liaison between the committee and the board.

The chairperson must be prepared to invest a substantial amount of time in the selection process. This was vividly expressed by the chairperson of the committee of a small liberal arts college where the process lasted five months and included the services of outside consultants: "But I won't take the job of chairman again. I had to work at it 40 hours a week about two and a half months and I had damn good administrative help."

Another chairperson of a similar institution, which took seven months for its search and did not use outside help, wrote: "I think it necessary that one person have the time and interest to work on such a project. I personally attended all the committee meetings, all of the interviews, and made all of the telephone calls. In this effort, I traveled about 5,000 miles and spent 33 full days away from my home. I list these statistics only to point out that this experience was one of the most gratifying I have ever had. It has been successful, and I would not change one minute of it."

The board in setting up the search and selection committee(s) should also designate the chairperson. Where there are two committees, it is not uncommon for a faculty member to chair the search committee and a trustee to chair the selection or screening committee, thus reflecting the relative influence of the two groups in their respective committees.

Committee Staff and Office

The selection of a president involves for most institutions, public and private, four-year and two-year, a considerable amount of grubby detail. Committee meetings must be scheduled and often rescheduled. Mailing lists must be prepared. Letters must go out inviting nominations and advertisements placed in appropriate newspapers and journals. Responses must be acknowledged, background data on candidates collected, an efficient filing system established. Interviews must be arranged, travel schedules set up, expenses approved and paid. These are not the proper function of committee members who donate their time.

The sensible committee will, at the very start of its operations, arrange for adequate and responsible staff assistance. In most situations, this means a staff officer or administrative secretary who knows how to be discreet and who preferably can give full time to the assignment for the duration. It should be someone who knows the institution and who is respected by the various constituencies. Sometimes an administrative officer of the institution (not remotely in the line of succession!) can serve the committee on a part-time basis. In either case, varying amounts of clerical help will be needed, especially at times of peak load in correspondence. All members of the committee's staff must be carefully selected, for they will be under pressure from the academic community and the press for information.

The committee will need a room where files can be safely kept and where the staff officer can receive, sort, and answer mail. Ideally, the room should be large enough for comfortable committee meetings and conferences for two or more members.

To protect confidentiality and for other reasons, some comittees have employed outside consulting firms to handle administrative details. Occasionally, the chairperson will run the show from his or her own office to safeguard confidentiality or to save the college money or simply for convenience. Some institutions establish off-campus offices as a security precaution. However it is done, the lesson is clear: the job of selecting a president is too important to skimp on staff.

Timetable

Selection committees, like legislatures, tend to start slow and end in a rush. It is not just that the final deadline seems at first a comfortable distance away; committees frequently underrate the time required and the cumulative impact of inevitable delays. Therefore, it is important for the committee to set a realistic schedule for itself at the start of its operations. This should allow for the time necessary to organize, to send out letters inviting nominations, to place advertisements with a cutoff date for replies, to screen the *curricula vitae* of 50 to 500 candidates, to check references of perhaps 15 to 20, to arrange preliminary interviews with perhaps 10 to 15 and campus visits for the final 3 to 5, to make final checks on the survivors, and to reach agreement on the candidates to be recommended to the board.

In its charge to the committee the board should set the date, usually one of its regularly scheduled meetings, at which it expects to take action on the committee's recommendations. This date should be early enough to permit the president-elect to take over from the outgoing incumbent without an interregnum (except in crisis situations) and to allow for some additional margin of time in case the committee or board cannot agree on a candidate or if the candidate agreed on declines to accept. Given its deadline, the committee should work backwards in setting its timetable.

How long will the search and selection process take? This varies greatly from one institution to the next, depending on the nature of the transition and the point in the academic calendar at which the search takes place. As the following table shows, universities, whether public or private, tend to take a longer time and two-year colleges, private as well as public, the least time. Another generalization to be drawn from the table is that public institutions on the whole take less time than private institutions. Twelve months was the longest time reported in our survey by a public institution, whereas it took some private four-year institutions 18 months, and one private junior college 24.

In the study by Judith McLaughlin referred to in Chapter 1, we get the time schedules indicated on the next page.

It all goes to show how difficult it is to establish a common pattern.

Universities, being large and complex organizations, generally require more time. The not infrequent restrictions on choice in church-related colleges can shorten the process. In the extreme example of a four-year church-related institution requiring only one

	Range	Median
4-year public	2–12 months	7.5
2-year public	1–6 months	4.5
private university	1–18 months	9.0
4-year private	4–18 months	7.0
4-year church-related	1 day–15 months	5.7
2-year private	3–24 months	5.0

	1–6 months	7–9 months	11–12 months
Public institutions	11	4	5
Private institutions	16	7	3

day to select a president (see the table), a committee of six trustees and three faculty members met for one evening only, reviewed the credentials of the ten eligible individuals and agreed in short order to nominate one.

The chairperson of another church-related college committee, which spent four months reviewing 85 candidates, commented: "In my opinion, a search committee can spend too much time on a search. Deadlines must be established and met." Most committees would be happy if their labors could be limited to four months. How long is enough will depend in part on local circumstances, in part on the efficiency of the committee. Bolman is probably correct in cautioning that after a year exhaustion tends to set in.[2] In addition, the best candidates will be lost to other institutions. Four to six months should suffice.

While the search continues, the amount of time required from committee members is considerable. Weekly or fortnightly meetings for long periods of time are not uncommon. In one community college where the entire board of seven served as the search committee, the number of meetings averaged between two and three per week for a period of five months. While this is an extreme situation, committee members should understand that they are undertaking a time-consuming, as well as important task.

Exhibits A and B contain sample time-tables, one of four months' and the other of eight months' duration.[3]

Use of Consultants

Sooner or later the search committee must decide whether to employ outside professional help. This can range from using one or more consultants—usually ex-administrators or faculty members whose specialty is educational administration—to relying on a management consulting firm. Some of the major commercial firms, which have made their reputations identifying top officers for business enterprises, now include similar services for non-profit organizations. In recent years a new family of consulting firms designed to provide a variety of services to educational institutions has come into being. Among them are specialists in the recruitment of top academic officers.

In our survey 20% of the respondents employed professional firms or individual consultants to assist in the selection process—10% of the public colleges and universities and 24% of the private institutions. Two-year colleges seemed more inclined to seek outside help than did four-year institutions (27% of community colleges, 43% of private junior colleges). These figures would be higher today.

Outside consultants and professional firms were used, according to our respondents, for a variety of purposes: (1) to advise and assist in setting up the committee's procedures, (2) to help define the institution's needs and establish desirable criteria, (3) to develop a pool of candidates, (4) to screen the candidate roster, (5) to conduct interviews, (6) to make site visits and in other ways to check up on finalists, and (7) even — incredible as it may seem—to participate in the final evaluation and recommendation.

Since the search for college and university presidents is becoming increasingly difficult and complex, why did 80% of the institutions in our survey not make use of competent professional help? It has not been part of the academic tradition, so runs one answer. But that tradition is clearly changing. Faculty, and to a lesser extent trustees, have an instinctive distrust of the outsider who is an alien, who cannot be expected to understand and appreciate the special quality of "our" college, and who is sometimes suspected of wanting to manipulate the process in favor of a predetermined candidate. These myths and prejudices erode slowly.

Expense is another factor. While the cost of individual educational consultants on a *per diem* basis can be quite modest, consulting firms are more expensive. Major business-oriented management companies charge 30 to 33% of the first year's salary of the appointee; nonprofit consulting firms can run as high as $15,000 to $18,000 depending on the amount of work involved. In one state university the outside fee represented $12,500 of a total cost of $32,000, and the fee paid by a community college in the far west must have constituted a significant part of the $50,000 total cost for a two and a half month search. If the right person is found, however, the fee has been a good investment.

In many cases, trustees and faculty members believe they have sufficient competence to run their own show. In most statewide systems the central office has one or more administrators whose job it is to assist member colleges or universities in choosing new presidents and who often maintain a current roster of potential candidates. Their involvement in frequent searches provides a background of experience that often obviates the need for outside help. Some private colleges will have on their boards one or more trustees who have been through the process before and who are prepared to play an active role a second time. But this is the exception rather than the rule.

"The increased use of consultants to assist in searches for presidents (as well as, of course, searches for other top administrators) reflects the growing appreciation of greater complexities in many sectors of higher education, and the dawning recognition that recruiting suitable candidates for a position exposed to unusual stress may neither be plain sailing in procedural terms nor terms of optimal outcome."[4] The chief thrust of the Riesman/McLaughlin argument comes from their conviction that increasingly in the future good presidential candidates will need to be sought out and wooed. There will always be lots of aspirants to the position, but really good candidates will not apply. They are the ones who already have good positions and who will be most offended (and possibly damaged) by premature publicity. Consultants can be especially helpful in identifying and negotiating with such individuals.

There are, of course, other reasons for turning to professional assistance. An outside consultant can be of great value in a crisis situation where an institution has had two or more presidents in rapid succession, where the departure of the president to be replaced has been a stormy or unhappy one, or where feelings of distrust and antagonism affect the attitudes of faculty, students, and trustees. Where committees are or feel inexperienced, and a little fearful of proceeding alone, the experienced consultant can provide direction and support. When done by a consultant, the delicate and diplomatic background checking on the finalists before the committee makes its recommendation is generally more skillful and in less danger of premature disclosure.

Search committees, as we have noted, can choose from a considerable variety of commercial consulting firms. Among the non-profit agencies are the Academy for Educational Development with headquarters in New York City and Educational and Health Career Services located in Princeton. The most widely used, however, is the Presidential Search and Assessment Service (PSAS) established jointly by the Association of Governing Boards of Universities and Colleges and by the Association of American Colleges. It operates out of Washington, D.C., and its two consultants are both experienced administrators. PSAS is prepared to work with boards and their search committees from start to finish or to assist in certain more limited tasks. Its relatively modest scale of fees is determined by the work involved.

The Cost of a Search

From the responses to our survey, it proved difficult to get accurate figures on the cost of selecting a new president. Some institutions included in their cost figures *pro rata* salaries of administrative officers and staff secretaries; others omitted these and listed only the more obvious out-of-pocket expenses occasioned by committee travel and bringing candidates to the campus. Two small church-related colleges claimed no official expense on grounds that the committee members paid their own expenses. One must surmise that they either did not bring any candidates to be interviewed on campus or required them to pay their own expenses, neither of which is a practice to be recommended. The time donated by committee members is of course a real, albeit unrecorded, cost to the members.

Consider the costs involved in a search: one administrative agent, full or part-time; one clerical secretary (and at certain peak periods two); advertising in public media; stationery; postage; filing cabinets; telephone; committee travel and meals; candidate travel, housing, and meals; and the fees of outside consultants if used. This last item can be substantial, as noted in the preceding section. Trustees may donate their own travel expenses along with their services, but it is not reasonable to expect other committee members to do so, and it is certainly not desirable to ask candidates to pay their own way.

For what limited guidance they may provide, here are the cost ranges reported by our correspondents:

4-year public	$1,000–25,000
2-year public	0—50,000
private university	2,000—55,000

4-year private college	0—50,000
4-year church-related	0—25,000
2-year private	0— 5,000

It must be obvious that with the exception of the one-evening selection process mentioned earlier in this chapter, every search and selection process costs something. It should also be noted that these are 1976-77 figures and would be higher today. Any extensive search (excluding those situations where the field of available candidates is limited) will probably cost not less than $25,000. Large universities or institutions using the more expensive type of business consultant might pay as much as $75,000. See Exhibit C for a sample search budget. It cannot be emphasized too strongly that the selection of the new president is so vital to the life of the institution—and the selection of the wrong one so disastrous—that this is no place to risk failure through false economy.

Some committees are instructed to do whatever is necessary and not to worry about the cost; the college or university will pick up the tab. At the other extreme is the dangerous assumption by the board or by the committee that the job must be done at minimal cost by cutting corners and overworking staff. Most committees will find it more comfortable to calculate in advance a budget of expenses and to know that there are sufficient funds to cover them. If funds are not available, for example, for 15 preliminary interviews, or ten on-site investigations by members of the committee or five campus visits by final candidates and their spouses, the program must be tailored

accordingly. Those numbers, however, come close to being the minimum for a well-conducted search—and any other kind is not worth doing.

Paperwork and Record Keeping

The normal search and selection process generates a substantial mass of documents. In addition to hundreds of letters and memoranda announcing the vacancy and inviting nominations or applications, there will be the documents providing information on 50 to as many as 300 candidates. For each there needs to be a dossier containing biographical information and correspondence; and for those who survive the early screening process, there will be letters of reference, reports on conversations, telephone calls, and interviews.

Some committees make copies of all documents for each member of the committee, accepting the not inconsiderable cost of doing so and also the very real risk that the sensitive and confidential information may inadvertently find its way into the wrong hands. Other committees, for reasons of economy or security, maintain a central office and file to which only members and staff have access and where they can do their homework. This is manageable where much of the screening is done by campus members of the committee, but under most circumstances it imposes an additional burden on already overworked trustee members.

Difficult choices among individuals being considered for the same job will sometimes erupt in controversy, with angry accusations and unfounded rumors being spread to the detriment of all concerned. Furthermore, regulations regarding equal opportunity/affirmative action require those committees subject to such regulations to demonstrate by the record, if challenged, the legitimacy of their actions. The best defense in both situations is to maintain full and complete records of committee activities and decisions. This record should include minutes of meetings, the record of decisions respecting the status of candidates, memoranda regarding the substance of telephone conversations, memoranda summarizing the results of individual interviews, reports from subcommittee of investigations, reactions from members of the academic community to whom candidates have been exposed, and the like. The record should show how wide a net had been cast, and how many candidates were women and members of minority groups. The need for a complete record is also important for keeping the search process on the trolley tracks. Consideration of many candidates over a period of many weeks and even months breeds confusion. Memories become dim or erratic. The written record is the only sure safeguard.

The Problem of Confidentiality

Candidates for a presidency—a majority of them at least—would prefer that their candidacy be kept confidential. The campus community and the public press, on the other hand, want to know what is going on. The selection of a new president provides a classic example of the conflict between the individual's right to privacy and the public's right to know.

Much unhappiness and even bitterness have resulted from breaches of promised confidentiality on the one hand and refusal to give out any information on the other hand. Thus, it behooves every search committee to decide at the start of its operations how it will handle its public relations. Committees, of course, at public institutions in states with strong sunshine laws such as Florida and Minnesota must comply with statutory requirements. In those states everything must be done in full public view.

Some presidents prefer on principle to have everything out in the open.[5] Others for practical reasons think it preferable. "My candidacy was known to the campus community at the time of my initial visit," wrote a private university president. "Thus, I had opportunity to speak openly to faculty, staff, and students prior to my appointment. I liked it that way."

The majority of candidates, however, were either strongly opposed to having their candidacy discussed in public or were resigned to what they considered the inevitable. Those vehement in the defense of confidentiality pointed out that publicity jeopardizes the candidate's position or standing in his present institution (one said that he would have felt obliged to resign from his present position if he had not been selected), that public discussion of the merits of various candidates is almost always embarrassing to those not selected, and that the whole business of being on public display is distasteful.[6]

The breach of confidentiality occurs in two quite different ways. One is by leaks, which seem to be endemic in modern life and particularly to political situations. These occur most frequently where the departure of the last president left a troubled campus, where there are one or more internal candidates with their local supporters or critics, and where there is an aggressive press. About all one can do is to pledge members of the search and selection committee to complete secrecy (which, alas, too often fails to work), to announce that the finalists will be brought to the campus for public inspection, to report regularly and frequently on the progress of the search except for the names of candidates, and to review in advance how inquiries should be handled.

Two good rules to follow are: first, appoint a single spokesman for the committee, in most cases its chairperson; and, second, establish (at the start, if possible) good working relations with the media.

The composition of the committee, its mandate, the procedures it proposes to follow, its progress week by week are all matters of public interest and should be explained carefully to students, faculty, alumni, and the general public. Contacts should be established with the student newspaper, representatives of the public press and, where interested, with broadcasters for radio and television. One private university committee chairperson won the cooperation of the media by telling them frankly at the beginning of what proved to be a difficult and contentious search that premature public discussion of individual candidates would cause the university to lose some of its best prospects and that he would keep them fully informed of everything that went on or that they wanted to know except the identification of the candidates themselves.

In addition to leaks, the second way in which disclosure occurs is through the public visit to the campus by the finalists. Such visits need not be public, but it is difficult to prevent them from becoming so. Such visits serve the dual purpose of enabling local constituencies to see and size up the candidates, an exercise that is particularly important for faculty and administration, and to give the candidates a chance to appraise the institution and the groups that compose it. "Given the procedure used to select the president," wrote a state university president, "it would not have been possible to maintain confidentiality and at the same time to have open interviews by students and faculty on campus. I think the procedure is clearly more important than any benefits to be derived from confidentiality."[7]

In several states legislation mandates open meetings for all public bodies and committees. In most cases committees are permitted to go into executive session when sensitive matters are under discussion such as the consideration of candidates for a presidency; but in Florida and Minnesota everything must be done in full public view.

There are those who think that people in academic life are too sensitive about their position and person. Being public figures, they must learn like politicians to conduct their lives in public. "I was a known or declared candidate from the start," wrote a community college president in Florida. "I had to get 'in line' with 300 or so candidates and was in the finals with five others. I didn't have any idea about the outcome until the morning of the board meeting when a vote of 3 to 2 was cast in my favor. I prefer all things out in the open—in the long run facts get out anyway, usually distorted, so keep it in the sunshine."

The major disadvantages of such a procedure are two. First, it reduces the number of top candidates, for the best qualified individuals are often the least inclined to submit themselves to being dressed and undressed in public. The strongest candidates are most likely to have good jobs already. Indeed, as we shall see in Chapter IV, the best people are frequently reluctant candidates who need to be wooed rather than displayed on the auction block. Second, it lengthens the time necessary for screening and final selection. We shall discuss this in Chapter V, but, in brief, the necessity of comparing the qualifications of candidates in public requires caution, artifice, and circumlocution in time-consuming amounts.

Additional Sources of Information

Donald E. Fouts: "Picking a President the Business Way," *AGB Reports,* vol. 19, no. 1, January/February 1977.

Frederick deW. Bolman: "How Will You Find a College President?" *AGB Reports,* vol. 12, no. 7, April 1970.

_____ . *How College Presidents Are Chosen,* American Council on Education 1965.

Richard A. Kaplowitz: *Selecting Academic Administrators: The Search Committee,* American Council on Education 1973.

Joseph F. Kauffman: *The Selection of College and University Presidents,* Association of American Colleges 1974.

Sam P. Kelly: "The Administrative Hiring Process," *Liberal Education,* vol. 43 no.3, October 1977.

Richard Sommerfeld and Donna Nagely: "Search and Ye Shall Find," *Journal of Higher Education,* vol. 45, no. 4, April 1974.

Checklist #2
Organizing the Committee

Search committees at public institutions may need to organize themselves in a somewhat different fashion from those at private colleges and universities. Owing to bylaws or other formally adopted regulations, they may have less freedom of choice. Nevertheless, the similarities in organization and procedure are greater than the differences, and therefore the following checklist will be useful for public as well as private four-year as well as two-year, institutions.

1. Arrange for adequate staff. Universities, both public and private, will need more staff than community colleges and small private institutions. Universities should count on a full-time or nearly full-time administrative officer plus secretarial help. Community colleges and small private institutions can often manage with the part-time assistance of a college officer, but extra secretarial help will be needed at certain stages. Unless the search and selection are to be carried on in full public view, care should be taken to find supporting staff who in all ways will be thoroughly discreet.

2. Establish suitable offices for conducting the committee's business and protecting confidentiality of documents.

3. Establish a timetable with target dates for each stage. Allow leeway for delays and slip ups. The board should set the date on which it wants final recommendations.

4. Decide whether to use outside professional help—a decision that will depend in part on a judgment regarding the experience and competence of the committee or of the central office in statewide systems. Decide whether professional help will be used for one or more phases of the total operation, such as advice on procedure, developing a pool of candidates or investigating the backgrounds of top candidates, or throughout the search.

5. Set up a budget adequate to meet costs. The best advice is not to scrimp. The outcome is too important.

6. Maintain a complete record of the entire search and selection process. Equal opportunity/affirmative action regulations require such a record for institutions with substantial government contracts. The possibility of charges of favoritism, and in extreme cases of lawsuits, makes a written record highly desirable. Decide at the start what should be included—minutes of meetings, decisions, memoranda on interviews and telephone calls. Such a record is more important for public institutions than for private, because the former have to operate more in the pubic domain.

7. Decide how much confidentiality is desired: (1) complete till final announcement, (2) until campus visits of finalists, or (3) none at all. Review the danger of leaks and guard against them. Work out a program of public information. Seek cooperation of the media. Decide on a spokesman for the committee—presumably the chairperson.

1. What is said of a single committee is equally applicable to situations involving multiple committees. In this chapter and elsewhere, unless specifically noted, we shall ignore those exceptional situations where no real search occurs and selection is made in one or two meetings. Such situations infrequently occur, sometimes because the choice is restricted by charter to the members of a religious group, sometimes because an administrative officer or trustee has been groomed for the job or is so clearly everyone's choice that a general search is considered superfluous. Some of the "inside" presidents in our survey, however, indicated a certain amount of discomfort over being chosen without any real competition.

2. Frederick deW. Bolman: "How will You Find a College President?", *AGB Reports*, vol. 12, no. 7, April 1970.

3. The American Council on Education published in 1973 a useful study on search and selection procedures by Richard A. Kaplowitz of Rutgers University (29 pages). The timetable and flow chart of committees are of particular interest.

4. David Riesman and Judith Block McLaughlin in "Executive Recruiters in Search for College Presidents," unpublished paper 1983. This is a thoughtful and illuminating analysis of the dangers and advantages of using outside consultants; it concludes: "Altogether, we think it likely that more and more institutions searching for presidents will employ consultants. . . . Employing a search consultant is certainly no guarantee of success. An inexperienced consultant can cause as many problems as he or she solves. But an experienced consultant, carefully chosen by the search committee, can greatly facilitate the institution's most critical act, the selection of a new president."

5. One state college president reported that lack of confidentiality "created no problem for me. I prefer the public meeting and action only at public meetings."

6. One state university president whose selection was held in the open, reported: "I would not go through that process again." On the other hand, a state college president in a sunshine-law state, wrote: "Personally, I think that my interview went better because the final session was a public interview. By that time, I had experienced so many small groups and one-person interviews in the process that it was refreshing to have a change—even if it was open to the public."

7. In this section, I am greatly indebted to Judith Block McLaughlin, whose doctoral thesis at Harvard entitled *Confidentiality and Disclosure in the Presidential Search* is the best treatment of the subject with which I am familiar.

Chapter 3

Step Three—
Formulating
the Criteria

T he objective of the presidential selection process is the matching of a person and an institution, so that one meets the other's needs at a particular moment in history. A president who might have been an institution's savior 20 years ago may bring about its ruin today. Or a man who would be ideal at the helm of one college or university might nearly cause a shipwreck at another."[1]

The Board's Responsibility

Chapter 1 began with the propositions: (1) that the selection of the new president is the responsibility, indeed a major responsibility, of the board of trustees; (2) that the board must, therefore, determine the criteria

by which the new president will be chosen; and (3) that these criteria should be derived from an analysis of institutional objectives and needs over the next ten years.

Some boards, especially among community colleges, will themselves undertake the institutional analysis and/or formulate the qualities that the new president should possess. If wise, they will invite the participation of the campus community. Some boards, faced with a change in administration, will turn to the academic community for a quick fix on institutional goals and problems, from which a list of presidential characteristics can be derived. These are then modified or endorsed by the board and given to the selection committee as part of its official mandate. A few boards find themselves in the fortunate situation of having just completed some long-range plans or the kind of institutional appraisal required for reaccreditation.

In a majority of cases, however, the formulation of criteria is part of the mandate to the search and selection committee or occasionally, where there is more than one committee, to the advisory committees. A few committees reporting in our survey referred their conclusions back to the board for official approval, and at one state university the committee published its tentative criteria for the new president, held day-long public hearings at which anyone could object or make suggestions, and then settled on the final version knowing that there was substantial agreement within the university community.

It should be pointed out here, however, as it was in Chapter 1, that the future course of an institution is a matter that must be agreed upon by the whole board after careful study.

The Institutional Analysis

The practice of deriving presidential criteria from an appraisal of an institution's present condition and future prospects is approved in theory and largely ignored in practice. Both boards and the search committees they appoint have a tendency to rush into the search and selection of candidates without taking adequate stock of what or whom they really need. One of the important lessons that committees still need to learn is the desirability of examining the problems and prospects of their institutions *before* deciding what kind of individual endowed with what kind of talents will cope most successfully with those problems over the com-

ing decade.

This is very well put by Judith McLaughlin and David Riesman in another collaborative essay (to be published in the *Review of Higher Education*) entitled "The Vicissitudes of the Search Process": "If a successful search is to be conducted, the search committee must have a clear sense of the sort of person for whom they are searching. The starting point of the search process, then, should be introspection concerning what the institution needs in order to reorganize strengths and to cope with weaknesses, both in terms of history and tradition, and future prospects and dilemmas. . . . Without an institutional assessment and leadership definition, the search committee is also at a loss to know who will be the best choice for them. They run the risk of choosing someone totally inappropriate for their institution, someone whose attractiveness lies in the fact that his or her style differs from the departing president, or someone whose understanding of the college or university is too limited for effective leadership."

How should the trustees or the search and selection committee go about the business of taking institutional stock? There is rarely time for the elaborate type of self-study that boards might well authorize at less critical moments. One needs to know something about the present condition of the college or university, about the problems looming on the academic horizon if not already present, and about the direction in which the institution must go to maintain its position or enhance its reputation, to improve its services, or even merely to stay alive. This is a stage at which competent and educational-ly experienced consultants can be of great value.

Here is a checklist of areas and issues common to public and private, four-year and two-year, institutions, though not necessarily applicable in full to any one of them.

1. Changes in objectives. Is the college or university at a point in its history where it either wants or needs to change its direction, i.e., its goals and purposes? Community colleges do adjust to changes in the social-political-industrial character of their environment. State normal schools seek full-spectrum university status. Many church-founded colleges have evolved at some point into independent institutions.

2. Fiscal management. In an era of limited if not actually declining resources, is the institution in a relatively strong, weak, or middling position? Is the business office well equipped to cope, or must the new president be prepared to shore up crumbling financial control?

3. Educational expansion. Is the institution under pressure to expand into new areas, or do faculty and trustees believe that such expansion would be desirable? Community colleges are almost always under pressure by sectors in the community to add vocational courses. Liberal arts colleges get student pressure for more business courses and overseas programs. A southern state university has just made the major plunge into a medical school, and an eastern institution is going into veterinary medicine.

4. Consolidation of educational programs. What some institutions need is not to expand, but to pull in their horns. Has the proliferation over years of courses, depart-

ments, schools, centers, institutes weakened the capacity to survive? The president who can lead the institution into new areas and programs has a different temperament and different attributes from the president who can manage retrenchment and consolidation.

5. Enrollment. What are the institution's enrollment prospects? Should an aggressive recruitment program be launched? Are there new sources of students? What changes in age, sex, background of the student body are likely? What changes are desirable?

6. Educational quality. Is it high, so that the only issue is to keep it that way? Is it good and, therefore, not a major focus of effort? Is it less than what it ought to be? If so, is the problem primarily one of the quality of the student body or the quality of the faculty or the kind of values that permeate the institution? If improving the quality of the educational program is the central problem, the new president should have certain intellectual and personal qualities that will fit him or her for the kind of leadership required.

7. Physical plant. How adequate are the library, laboratories, classrooms, dormitories, athletic facilities, and social centers for the desired size and character of the institution? Must a major effort be made to add new buildings or to renovate buildings that have been allowed to deteriorate? Some individuals find creative pleasure in building buildings and in improving old ones. Others have interests focused on quite different ends.

8. Collective bargaining. Although faculty unions are more common in public

25

than in private institutions, they are a relatively new phenomenon in academic administration, and no college or university can be confident of being exempt. What will be the new president's attitude toward collective bargaining? How effective will he or she be in dealing with the union if one exists on campus? If one is being considered, will the new president try to stave it off or welcome it? The board's and faculty's own attitudes toward this issue are likely to incline them toward one candidate rather than another.

9. Student life and activities. These will vary enormously from non-residential community colleges to private or church-related colleges where virtually all the students reside in dormitories. But every educational institution provides some extracurricular programs ranging from counseling to sports to social activities. How adequate is this phase of the institution's total operation? Where should it be improved? Is this a major concern, sufficiently important to influence the choice of the new president?

10. Governance. Does it work well? Do the various constituencies have a voice in it, and are they satisfied? Is there pressure for change? Should the new president have the kind of political savvy necessary for a successful reorganization of the governing structure?

11. Self-image. How does the institution see itself? Is it satisfied with its image? This is a subtle matter of morale and institutional esprit.

Public institutions face problems that private colleges and universities do not, and vice versa. Community colleges with their close ties to local communities, have different objectives and problems. In making a quick survey of where the institution stands and what its goals and needs will be over the next decade, trustees and committee members will want to examine the following.

Public Four-Year Colleges and Universities

1. External relations. What is the place and status of the institution with respect to (a) the central office of the statewide system and (b) the governor, the educational commissioner, and the legislature? Do communications need to be improved? Do the external relations need major attention in order for the college or university to hold its own or improve its relative position?

2. Regional economy. Is the state's population growing or declining? In what ways is the economy likely to change? What new demands or pressures will the university experience?

3. Multicampus problems. How do local educational units relate to the central system office? Are changes likely to occur in this relationship? Will new units be added or existing ones closed? What political forces will affect decisions?

4. Autonomy. Closely related to the above is the degree of autonomy the institution enjoys. In what areas and to what extent can the trustees and administration make their own decisions regarding programs, plant, salary levels, and the like? How much political interference does the university suffer? Is the situation healthy or is a major battle looming over the autonomy of the institution?

5. *Consolidation of control.* While consolidation of programs is a question for all types of institutions, central control over the often semi-independent fiefdoms of the academic world is a special issue for large state universities with their extensive range of programs and services. Is the university a reasonably unified whole, as the term "university" implies that it should be, or is there a problem here with which the president must deal?

6. *Equal opportunity.* Many state institutions are struggling with the problems generated by federal and state regulations respecting equal opportunity/affirmative action. This impinges on the college or university both at the hiring level—especially faculty—and the recruitment of students. Have the university's procedures been worked out or is the major crunch still ahead? Has the institution moved to open admissions? If not, will it be forced to in the near future, and what kind of problems will that produce?

7. *Athletics.* Does the university have a sensible and defensible athletic program? Is there public and alumni pressure for bigger and better football or basketball teams? Do these sports play a disproportionate role in the institution's life and budget? Is the director of athletics king in his own castle, controlling funds and programs over which the administration has no voice?

Private Colleges and Universities

1. *Sense of mission.* Important for all types of institutions, but particularly critical for the private college. Is the campus har-

monious? Do faculty and administration and trustees work well together? Or is there antagonism and political infighting? Have recent issues exacerbated the situation? Must the new president provide charismatic leadership? Does the institution need someone who can help the board become more effective and involved?

2. *Student recruitment.* Does the institution face difficulties in maintaining a satisfactory number of applicants? How will conditions over the next decade affect student recruitment? What steps will need to be taken? Is the problem one of better public relations or better organization of the admissions office and procedures? What does this say about the kind of person who should be president?

3. *Quality of faculty.* While the improvement of educational quality is a question for the trustees of all institutions, the size and quality of the faculty is frequently an urgent problem for the private college. What is and what should be the student-faculty ratio? Is the faculty too large or too small? Does it need upgrading? What steps might be taken?

4. *New clienteles.* Can and should the college or university compensate for the dwindling pool of 17 to 21 year-old students by recruiting older people? What changes in programs would this involve?

5. *Public relations.* How is the institution viewed in the surrounding community, by alumni, donors, and friends? Does the institutional image need improvement? Do alienated alumni and friends need to be wooed back? Are there new publics the college should seek to interest?

6. *Church relations.* For church-related colleges relations with the founding and/or sponsoring denominations constitute a special area of concern. Is the problem one of rekindling church or denominational interest and support; or is it one of reducing the influence and control of the denomination that supports the institution?

Community Colleges

1. Community needs. Because community colleges are local institutions serving primarily local needs, they have a special obligation to be responsive to changing community needs. What is happening to the community? What kind of programs will serve it best in the next ten years? Is the problem one of consolidation and growth or of radical redirection?

2. Expansion. Community colleges have been the fastest growing segment of postsecondary education. Should there be and can there be limits to further growth? Should expansion be concentrated on one campus, or should multiple campuses be developed?

3. Physical plant. Since community colleges have been the most recent development in American higher education, many of them have not had time or money to develop adequate physical facilities for their rapidly increasing enrollments. Is physical growth, even a change in location, going to be a major problem in the next few years? Some people will relish the opportunity; others will look upon it as a necessary evil. The choice of the new president will determine how well and enthusiastically it is done.

4. Financial crunch. The difficult times that affect all colleges and universities bear particularly heavily on the community colleges. Periodic attempts at tax reform reflect citizen attitudes. The dependence of community colleges on local and state tax revenues makes them vulnerable. To what extent will the issue be one of holding the line or effecting reductions in budget? How important is someone with a keen eye for figures and a sharp pencil?

5. Community support. The goodwill of the local community is essential to the community college. Does the college have a problem? Does the community image need refurbishing? Does it have the wholehearted support of community sponsors? How much attention will the new president need to give to this area?

6. Politics. As with public four-year institutions, community colleges must expect a high degree of public interest and often a considerable amount of public interference or attempted interference. Where community colleges are members of a statewide system, they face the same problems of autonomy that state universities face. Is the working relation between the central state office and the local college satisfactory? Do state or county or quite local politics limit the college's freedom? How can political interference be kept to a minimum? If these are serious problems, it says something very important about the kind of man or woman who should be invited to cope with them.

The Presidential Profile

There are some qualities that any president should have: an understanding of what education is all about, a reasonable degree of administrative ability, the physical and emotional stamina to work long hours frequently under considerable stress, and, above all, those moral ingredients of leadership such as honesty, courage, and personal integrity.[2]

Committees are inclined to draw up list specifying age range, marital status, degrees, experience, religious affiliation, and the like. These can sometimes become embarrassing when the best candidate fails to meet some of the specifications, e.g., a doctor's degree. They can also become so absurd in their delineation of the ideal president that the reader either laughs or winces according to his or her temperament.[3]

The real test of intelligent criteria is their relevance to the current and future condition of the college or university. What is its mission for the next ten years? Where are its major problems? Does it need an educator, a fund raiser, or a caretaker? Should the new president be like the old or quite different?[4]

Committees need to steel themselves against the danger of preconceived ideas of what a president should look and act like. The candidate who has no enemies has probably never done anything significant. We noted in Chapter 1 that diverse selection committees run the risk of ending up with bland personalities. Colleges and universities need presidents of character and conviction, and committees should be prepared to look for nonconventional individuals, even controversial characters. The point has already been made that extra efforts should be made to find qualified women and members of minority groups. As Kauffman trenchantly states: "Search committee members must be vigilant that getting 'nice' people does not become the principal dynamic in the screening and assessment process."[5]

Most respondents to our survey stated that their search was based on an analysis of institutional needs. One committee spent two months on the analysis. Another held a retreat of several days. A third set up a two-day workshop, bringing in four different types of college presidents to help in a discussion of priority needs and variations in presidential profiles. One committee chairman, who said his institution did indeed complete a needs analysis, added: "My reservations are that we spent so much time on this that the search process itself suffered. By the time we felt good internal communications, trust, etc. had been been established, the pressures (both of time and patience) for a speedy choice were high. At least for an institution which had not attended to 'self-examination' very well before the search, a year on that and a year on the search would have been ideal."

The responses would be more impressive if the comments accompanying many of them did not suggest a less careful procedure. "We *all* seemed to know what we needed; eventually, at least," wrote the chairperson of a community college. The chairperson of a church-related college indicated that the committee had reversed the usual sequence. "When we established the criteria for our new president, we, in effect, also established the mission and future needs of the institution." The candid confession of the committee chairperson of an eastern woman's college is probably applicable to a good many committees: "The Committee *thought* at the time that it undertook an adequate review of these matters. In retrospect, and in the light of the examination of these questions that were undertaken during the two years since the new president took office, our examination at the time the search began was a bit superficial."

Some assessment of the institution's present and future prospects and problems along lines suggested in the preceding section should provide all-important clues to the kind of president needed. On the basis of such an analysis, it is possible to draw up a list of needed and desirable qualifications. Exhibits D and E offer two actual examples, one of an institutional analysis and the other of a presidential profile. Each committee will want to develop its own profile.

It is important, however, that the results of the analysis and the criteria built upon it be shared with all members of the academic community — trustees, faculty, students, administrative staff, alumni, patrons, and friends. There ought to be—one is tempted to say, there *must* be — widespread agreement prior to adoption in final form. The criteria should be published, and dissent should be given careful consideration. We have already seen earlier in this chapter how one state university committee held public hearings to provide feedback from the community. By getting the criteria out in the open, differences of opinion can be reconciled before they become entrenched. The process of reaching agreement enhances the sense of unity within the institution.

And in the end, agreement on criteria provides a platform of support for the new president. He or she will need it. High priority candidates and even presidents-elect can be killed off before taking office by angry faculty or strong-minded trustees, not because the candidates or presidents-elect do not meet the specifications, but because there never was agreement on what the specifications should be.

This is trenchantly put by the chairman of the selection committee of an eastern college: "To get the support of all the constituencies, we asked faculty, administration, students, alumni, and board members for their ideas on the future of the university and the qualifications of the new president. The response was excellent, and this was summarized on a page for each subject. The purpose here was to generate support from possible divergent interests and to provide a unifying pair of documents which would make sure that the choice finally arrived at would not be dead on arrival."

Checklist #3
Formulating the Criteria

1. Who will decide on the criteria by which the new president will be chosen?

2. Where does an institution begin with an assessment of present and future institutional needs? What questions should be asked?

    a. for any and every college and university;

    b. for public four-year institutions;

    c. for private colleges and universities;

    d. for community colleges?

3. What steps will best ensure agreement on institutional needs and presidential criteria?

4. Has the committee established a set of criteria for the new president based on an analysis of the institution's needs and problems in the next decade?

1. Frederick deW. Bolman: *How College Presidents are Chosen,* American Council on Education 1965, pp. 1-2.

2. Robert L. Strider, President Emeritus of Colby College, offers a thoughtful set of personal characteristics in "Memo to a Search Committee," *AGB Reports*, vol. 23, no. 1, January/February 1981.

3. A Yale trustee is alleged to have said during a presidential search that the man they were looking for "had to be a leader, a magnificent speaker and great writer, a good public relations man and fundraiser, a man of iron health and stamina, married to a paragon, a man of the world but with great spiritual qualities, an experienced administrator who can delegate authority, a Yale man and a great scholar. After lengthy deliberation we concluded that there was only one such person. But then a dark thought crossed our minds. Is God a Yale man?"

4. Committees occasionally make the mistake of seeking someone with qualities opposite to those of the outgoing president instead of basing their decision on objective analysis of institutional needs.

5. Joseph F. Kauffman: *At the Pleasure of the Board.* American Council on Education 1980, p. 26.

Chapter 4

Step Four—
Developing a Pool of
Candidates

Once the criteria for the presidency have been established, the next step is to develp a roster of candidates.[1] Owing to the urgency of the situation or to the impatience of the committee, this step is sometimes begun before the criteria have been settled. When this happens, it complicates the job of screening candidates because individuals who do not fit the final specifications often are included.

There are two schools of thought about the size of the pool. One advocates a limited search for a *good* man or woman; the other favors a broad search for the *best* individual.

The Limited Search

The extreme example of the limited search is where, for all practical purposes, there is no search at all. Very occasionally a board of trustees or its chairperson or the outgoing president will have a handpicked candidate ready and available. This will usually be an internal candidate who has been groomed for the job. Slightly less extreme is the situation where the president must be a member of a religious order or denomination — a requirement that can sharply limit the number of possible candidates.

The proponents of the short list and the prompt offer to the first person who looks really good point out the waste of time, money, and human emotions in screening dossiers of people who are not viable candidates. Long lists almost always include incompetents with exalted notions of their abilities and oustanding public figures who by no stretch of the imagination would be interested in the presidency of Siwash or Midwest State.

"I recognize the legal and practical necessity of the open search," writes a former college and university president and trustee of several institutions, "but I feel that the processing of hundreds of dossiers is counter-productive. It is confusing and it drains energies that should somehow be directed to the few qualified candidates . . . . Somehow way must be found to permit the committee to identify and cultivate promising and realistic candidates and not to waste energy on deleting unpromising ones."

Furthermore, the longer the search and screening, the greater the danger of losing good candidates, who are likely to be sought after by other institutions or who become disaffected with the uncertainty caused by long delays. A member of the search committee of a church-related college reported: "Search was too long (10 months). Lost several good candidates due to delay. My personal view, probably not widely shared on the campus, is that the best candidate should be invited to the campus, and if an acceptable candidate, an immediate offer should be tendered."[2]

The Broad Search

How broad the search should be will depend, as we have noted, on the nature and circumstances of the institution. Major universities and colleges with national reputations will inevitably attract more candidates than lesser known regional and local institutions; but even among the latter, there usually are compelling reasons for a reasonably extensive canvass, although this is sometimes overdone owing to the mistaken view that a limited number will be

seen as derogatory. The advocates of the broad search offer the following arguments:

1. Trustees and committees want and seek not a just a good man or woman but the best individual for their particular situation. The well known saying that the good is the enemy of the best applies here. The role and influence of the president on the well-being of the institution are too central, too critical, to justify settling for anything less than the best person available.

2. The task of screening out unsuitable or unsatisfactory candidates is undoubtedly time-consuming, but if the screening process is well planned, it is not difficult to weed out the many who are unsuitable. It is more of a problem where the search and selection process must be conducted in the open and candidates cannot be so summarily disposed of as can be done when committee meetings are held in private.

3. As noted in the Introduction, current federal and state legislation requires, in certain situations, honest efforts to make vacancies known to women, blacks, and members of other minority groups and to include them in the pool of candidates.[3] Even where not required by law, colleges and universities will want to follow the principle of equal opportunity.

4. The broad search involves more people. Invitations to faculty, students, alumni, and local citizens to nominate candidates or to suggest possible names give the various groups a sense of participation in the outcome. Requests to educators, foundation officers, distinguished citizens, elected or appointed state and local officials will bring the institution to their attention, increase their

knowledge of it and, if done astutely, enhance the reputation of the institution.

Alluring as the short list and quick decision may be, the arguments favor selection from a larger rather than a smaller pool of candidates. Although our survey turned up examples of all kinds, the great majority developed a substantial roster. The figures are as follows:

	Range of Pool	Median Number
4-year public	20-400	216
2-year public	5-217	58
private university	79-500	217
4-year private college	50-500	240
4-year church-related	1-500	95
2-year private	1-152	99

Sources of Names

There are various ways of developing a pool of candidates. Most committees employ more than one; a few use them all.

1. The time-honored method is to announce the vacancy (by press release, notice in the campus news bulletin, story in the alumni magazine) and to write letters to a variety of individuals inviting them to nominate suitable candidates. Broadcast invitations can go to faculty, students, and alumni. Individual letters should be sent to selected educators, foundation officers, church leaders, government officials, heads of educational organizations, selected friends of the institution. The extent of the mailing will depend on the national or regional character of the institution, the availability of funds, and the degree of con-

cern on the part of committee members to canvass the field.[4]

Private colleges and universities tend to put more emphasis and value than do public institutions on nominations from people who know the college or university. While a few in our survey spoke favorably of the applicants who responded to the public advertisements, several found this method useless and many reported that nominations by knowledgeable individuals was by far their best source of candidates. Exhibits G and H contain two samples of typical letters inviting nominations. (The information accompanying these letters made clear that each institution is an affirmative action/equal opportunity employer.)

2. A second and concurrent approach is to advertise. There was a time when presidents, like ministers, were expected to receive "a call" to a new post. To apply for the position was considered quite improper. It is still true that many individuals—often the best—will not apply, either because they consider it presumptuous or because they are happily placed where they are. But the temper of the times is changing. Furthermore, the legal requirements of equal opportunity/affirmative action encourage, though they do not require, public solicitation of candidates. The easiest way is to run some ads.

According to our survey, the most widely used vehicles for public notices are *The Chronicle of Higher Education*, *The New York Times* (especially the Sunday edition), and the *Wall Street Journal*. *The Chronicle* seems to be the most effective, and the high costs of advertising in *The New York Times* and the *Wall Street Journal* raises questions as to their value. In addition, many committees made selective use of notices in local or regional newspapers, educational journals, church or denominational bulletins, and publications with specialized audiences. In most cases such advertisements generated a considerable number of applicants.

The community colleges in our survey relied heavily on public notices. Public four-year institutions found them a mixed bag. For some the results were "very satisfactory"; for others the applicants were largely unqualified.

The private institutions, with the occasional exceptions noted above, found the results of public notices to be "of minimal value." "Made a lot of work. Satisfied the 'pure' that we were searching. Produced not one finalist," was one committee chairperson's comment. Even so, the effect of advertising may be more useful than is immediately obvious. Public notices may well bring the opening to the attention of individuals who will not respond directly with an application, but who will find an appropriate way by which their names can be proposed to the committee.

3. The third avenue is a refinement or specialized form of public advertising. There are publications and organizations created to serve women, blacks, and other minority groups. The number of these publications has been increasing in recent years as a result of federal and state legislation. Some are of dubious value. Committees should look carefully into the record of publications and agencies asking for paid notices or offering assistance for a fee. Following this section is a list of names and addresses of a few agencies from which help can be sought to make certain that equal opportunity is being provided.

4. Finally, there are the consulting firms whose business it is to assist (for a fee) organizations to find personnel. Their role and value were discussed in Chapter 2, so little more needs to be said at this point. Some colleges and universities have found them useful in providing names of topflight candidates. Those designed to serve educational institutions, such as the Presidential Search and Assessment Service and the Academy for Educational Development, will be familiar with the academic world and therefore in a position to advise about who is available and who would be suitable for a given institution.

There is no value in a large roster of candidates unless the right candidates are included. The sources we have suggested above may produce the right candidates, but there is no guarantee, of course. Committees should not hesitate to use a personal approach, writing or preferably telephoning to well-placed friends of the institution and to individuals who ought to be on the list. Nor should committee members hesitate to mention their interest in other than the conventional white, male, middle-forties candidates. Women, members of minorities, and controversial figures do not get the attention they deserve—which is a loss to higher education.

Equal Opportunity Recruitment Sources

The following organizations are prepared to make recommendations of women and minority-group members for consideration by search and selection committees. Committees are urged to consult them (and any others known to the comittee) as well as presidents of women's colleges and of colleges with high minority enrollments.

For women

Office of Women in Higher Education
American Council on Education
Suite 800, One Dupont Circle
Washington, D.C. 20036
American Association of Women in Community and Junior Colleges
Suite 410, One Dupont Circle
Washington, D.C. 20036
American Association of University Women
2401 Virginia Avenue, N.W.
Washington, D.C. 20037
National Association for Women Deans, Administrators and Counselors
Suite 624A, 1625 Eye Street, N.W.
Washington, D.C. 20006

For minorities

United Negro College Fund, Inc.
500 East 62nd Street
New York, N.Y. 10021
National Association for Equal Opportunity in Higher Education
2243 Wisconsin Avenue, N.W.
Washington, D.C. 20007
Office for Advancement of Public Black Colleges
National Association of State Universities and Land Grant Colleges
Suite 710, One Dupont Circle
Washington, D.C. 20036

American Association of Higher Education Hispanic Caucus
Dr. Hector Garza, Chairperson
School of Graduate Affairs
Eastern Michigan University
Ypsilanti, Michigan 48197
National Network of Hispanic Women
c/o Sylvia Castillo
P.O. Box 4223
Stanford, California 94305

The Reluctant Candidate

A recurrent criticism of the selection process is that the search for candidates is inadequate. Bolman found in his study of 116 institutions twenty years ago that few of them were satisfied with the way in which the roster of potential candidates had been developed.[5] In our survey the need for more and better candidates was voiced by several chairpersons representing both public and private institutions.

It cannot be emphasized too strongly that many of the best candidates are unlikely to apply and need to be courted. They normally are already well set in good positions, and while they might be enticed to go elsewhere, they are in no hurry to do so. Furthermore, they usually have enough self-confidence to know that jobs will be seeking them rather than their seeking jobs.

Committees sometimes assume that anyone—well, almost anyone — would be flattered to be asked to head their college or university, and therefore fail to recognize the need to sell the position. This is often a delicate and sometimes a drawn out process. We have already pointed out in Chapter 2 the serious handicap that rigorous sunshine laws present to some committees. Sometimes committees create their own obstacles, such as asking individuals who have been nominated whether they are interested in applying for the job. A much better approach would be to ask if the committee could interest them in the position; or, if the individuals look like first-rate candidates, whether the committee might talk with them about possible candidates. Out of this conversation might develop a person's own interest in being considered.

This point is well stated by Donald E. Fouts in his article "Picking a President the Business Way." "The business search begins," he writes, "with the basic assumption that the ideal candidate is functioning successfully in his/her present position, not actively seeking new employment, and will probably not respond to advertisements or form-letter invitations to apply. Second, it is assumed that the search consultant has a responsibility to aggressively seek out such prospects and 'sell' them on the advantages of candidacy. Third, it is assumed that there is usually a direct relationship between the quality of the candidate and the amount of effort required to interest him/her in the position."[6]

This may overstate the case, but it would be difficult to overstate the need for the personal approach and for courting likely candidates both at this beginning stage and later when the committee is nearing the moment of truth.

The Inside Candidate

Reference has already been made to inside candidates. Because they are known to committee members and because they will have their strong advocates and quite possibly equally strong critics on campus, they present special problems to the committee.

If there are one or more *strong* internal candidates, and particularly if there is one obvious choice, it is tempting to short-circuit the elaborate search process. Time, money, and energy will be saved. Unless prohibited by law or by institutional bylaws, there is no obvious legal obstacle to promoting the provost, dean, or vice president without further ado.

There are, however, certain dangers and disadvantages in so quick a decision. The insider is likely to have worked long enough with the departing president to have adopted, if not his or her style, at least his or her philosophy of education and administration. This may not be what the college or university needs at that juncture in its history. Further, the institution loses the public relations value of a public search and the internal value of enhanced trust and good will among trustees, faculty, and students. And then there is the danger that the inside candidate may not be so much of a local hero as informal reports suggest. The search committee would be well advised to investigate the candidate's real standing with utmost care. It is the sort of thing an outside consultant can often do better than anyone on the inside.

If the committee decides, as most committees do, to carry through an open search, it must handle the inside candidate(s) with care and it must be prepared for trouble. To tell internal candidates that they will be treated like everyone else is easy; that indeed is the way they ought to be treated and in most cases will want to be treated. But their supporters will be eager on their behalf, and campus politics being what they are, special efforts will be made, tensions will rise, emotions will sometimes flare, and it will be hard to maintain confidentiality. If it turns out that inside candidates are not really in the running, it will probably save trouble to advise them of that fact as early as possible.

A strong inside candidate can also jeopardize the outside search. People who might normally be interested may suspect that the board search is a kind of charade and therefore decline to be considered. The committee may have to make an extra effort to convince outsiders that the search is wide open and on the level.

Correspondence

Preoccupation with screening and with the resulting short list of candidates leads many committees to neglect rank and file candidates. Sometimes months will go by without any communication from committee to candidates, who are concerned about making potential career, location, income, and family adjustments.

It is not only important, as a matter of courtesy, to acknowledge all applications, nominations, inquiries, and letters of reference, but also to maintain communication with candidates, nominators, and others actively involved. Letters should not be duplicated, but individually typed, even when a standard form is used.

Sensitive and personal treatment, even for those not in the running, will in the long run contribute to the reputation of the institution.

Additional Sources of Information

Frederick deW. Bolman: *How College Presidents are Chosen*, American Council on Education 1965.

Joseph F. Kauffman: *The Selection of College and University Presidents*, Association of American Colleges 1974.

Richard A. Kaplowitz: *Selecting Academic Administrators: The Search Committee*, American Council on Education 1973.

Donald E. Fouts: "Picking a President the Business Way," *AGB Reports*, vol. 19, no. 1, January/February 1977.

David J. Hanson and Cyrena N. Pondrum: *Guide to Federal Regulations*, National Association of College and University Business Officers 1974.

Checklist #4
Developing the Pool

1. Decide on the scope of the search for candidates.

    a. Broadly based or limited?

    b. National or regional?

    c. Restricted by religious requirement?

    d. Preference for a quick choice of a good person as soon as he or she appears?

2. Will the committee seek nominations or applications or both?

    a. How widely does the committee wish to send letters inviting nominations?

    b. Should the vacancy be advertised? Where?

3. What must the committee do to meet the requirements of equal opportunity/affirmative action?

4. Should outside professional services be used in generating names of candidates?

5. Each committee must decide whether to rely chiefly on those willing to apply (or ready to be considered) or to seek out the reluctant prospects and persuade them to consider the position.

6. How should the inside candidate be handled?

7. What procedures are necessary to make certain that there is no lapse in communication?

1. Throughout this study the term, *candidate*, is used to signify anyone who applies for the position, any individual who is nominated or proposed by a third party, or indeed anyone whose name comes before the committee for consideration.

2. Morton A. Raugh in *The Trusteeship of Colleges and Universities* (McGraw-Hill 1969) favors what he describes as "sequential selection." "In a task like this," he writes, "which involves searching and researching what in many cases may be hundreds of individuals, one can become obsessed with the idea that there is a single candidate clearly superior to any other and that somehow or other it can be determined just who the person is. It is not possible to predict with real certainty how good a man will be until he is observed functioning in the job. On this assumption, then, it makes sense to explore a limited list of prospects and consider choosing one of them if he shows good promise of meeting the requirements. The possibility that if you looked at enough people there might be a somewhat better candidate is ignored. If in the first batch there is no candidate considered suitable, a new roster is scanned." (pp. 16-17). See also Warren G. Bennis, *The Leaning Ivory Tower*, pp. 79-80, and Donald E. Fouts, "Picking a President the Business Way" (*AGB Reports*, vol. 19, no. 1, January/February 1977).

3. The legal requirements are set forth in Executive Order 11246, as Amended, Title VII of the Civil Rights Act of 1964, Title IX of the Education Amendments Act of 1972, and elsewhere. Both Joseph F. Kauffman in *The Selection of College and University Presidents* (Association of American Colleges 1974) and Richard A. Kaplowitz in *Selecting Academic Administrators: The Search Committee* (American Council on Education 1973) provide brief summaries of the regulations. A thorough analysis together with the relevant texts is to be found in the *Guide to Federal Regulations* (June 30, 1978) by David J. Hanson and Cyrena N. Pondrum, published by the National Association of College and University Business Officers. Committee members will find most useful the summary of the legal requirements prepared by John F. Zeller, Vice President and General Counsel of Bucknell University in connection with its most recent selection. The relevant sections are to be found in Exhibit F.

4. For example, the search committee chairperson of one church-related college reported: "In addition to the advertisements in *The New York Times* and *The Chronicle of Higher Education*, letters were written to all the state and federal representatives of the area, the heads of all the important foundations, the heads of all the important eastern universities as well as to all Lutheran colleges, the heads of all Lutheran synods in the United States, and to alumni, faculty and board members, asking for nominations." The search committee of a state university sent out more than 1,200 letters to the members of educational associations. Another state institution, however, reported that it declined to accept any nominations, apparently preferring to deal only with applicants in response to its advertisements.

5. Frederick deW. Bolman: *How College Presidents are Chosen*, American Council on Education, pp. 34-35.

6. Op. cit., p. 8.

Chapter 5

Step Five— Screening Candidates

A s soon as names begin to materialize in response to advertisements and invitations, the hard work of the committee or committees begins. Just how much work will depend on the size of the pool and the mandate to the committee.

At this stage the purpose is to select a limited and manageable number of likely candidates from the long roster of proposed names. The screening process is apt to stretch out over considerable time unless limits are set in advance. Two to three months should suffice. It is well to get started without delay on the business of sorting out candidates as their names come in.

Certain preliminary decisions, however, must be made. (1) What size should the eventual "select list" be? (2) Precisely who shall do the screening? (3) How extensive should be the committee's investigation of candidates?

(1) The Select List

The select list consists of those finalists judged by the committee to be worthy of serious consideration. The committee may decide to recommend to the board all candidates on the select list or to nominate one or more after further investigation. The list size will be dictated largely by the quality of the candidates.

A community college in the south requested its search and selection committee to present six names to the board. The mandate for many committees calls for three to five recommendations. Whatever the size planned by the committee, the list will probably end up with a different number.

The winnowing process is a continuous one, beginning almost as soon as the first names are presented to the committee. Some committees will be instructed to undertake preliminary screening only, with a second phase assigned to another committee or even assumed by the board itself. Other committees will have a mandate to continue screening until only a handful of first-rate individuals remain—the select list, in short.

Frederic W. Ness, veteran of many presidential searches, recommends that screening be thought of in three phases. In the first the list is reduced to 15-20, in the second to 8-10, in the third to those recommended to the board. The amount of information on which decisions are made will increase with each phase. The first reduction can be made fairly quickly on the basis of the usual kind of biographical data. More information from references and from the candidates will be necessary for the second reduction. Interviews should then be scheduled before the final or select list is recommended to the board.

Here, as in almost all matters pertaining to the search and selection process, it is important that committees adopt procedures suited to their situations. There are many good and bad practices, and the purpose of this manual is to encourage committees to follow the first and to help them avoid the second. Therefore, procedures that have proved successful in many circumstances are recommended, but they should be regarded as general guidelines and not as straightjackets.

(2) Who Does the Screening?

There are various ways of dividing up the work of screening. The first is not to divide it up at all, but to insist that every member of the committee read every dossier. Some committees believe quite strongly that this is the only proper way, but it means a large investment of man and woman hours. As the chairperson of one community college search committee reported: "Screening of about 130 candidates for a 14-member search committee takes far too much time. There should be a better way, but I cannot see how to do it and still involve all the necessary 'publics' to their satisfaction."

A second method is to divide the central committee into teams, each of which will read and rate its share of the dossiers. The subcommittees then report their tentative conclusions, which are adopted by the committee as a whole unless some member questions a decision to eliminate a candidate— in which case the candidate is kept on the active list. This seems to work quite well, especially where there is mutual trust among the committee members. Occasionally, there will be a feeling of uneasiness that different teams may use different standards of judgment, but a uniform rating system approved by the committee in advance should provide a fair measure of consistency.

A third route is the special screening committee. Some boards of trustees, as we have noted in Chapter 1, establish advisory committees of faculty, students, and staff. Several institutions in our survey, both public and private, assigned the preliminary screening function to these committees. A variation on this theme is to create a special screening committee or subcommittee composed of the faculty, staff, and student members of the search and selection committee. It is assumed tht faculty, staff, and students will have more time than trustees for the onerous work of sifting *curricula vitae* and readier access to the documents normally housed somewhere on campus.

This arrangement works, however, as with the previous method, only where there is great unity among the college or university constitutencies. Our survey produced many testimonies to this effect, but it also revealed the opposite. The example cited in Chapter 1 where a search and screening committee tried to take over responsibility for the final selection is a case in point. Consequently, some observers of the search and selection process argue strongly that there ought always to be one or more trustees involved in screening.

A fourth procedure is to assign the preliminary screening task to one individual—perhaps the chairperson (or in one case co-chairpersons) or the administrative staff person. This requires a high degree of confidence in one individual's judgment, even though that individual must present and defend his or her ratings before the whole committee.[1]

Finally, some committees make use of outside consultants to do the necessary screening. This saves the committee time and trouble. The screening is being done by a professional and that gives it a high probability of being well done. On the other hand, the professional consultant can be particularly helpful at the stage of intensive screening, whereas the committee can handle the preliminary screening and develop an important sense of teamwork in the process.

(3) How Extensive an Investigation?

One of the tricky points for screening operations is the kind of evidence on which preliminary decisions are made. How aggressive should committees be in seeking out data on candidates? The charge to the committee should make clear the limits to the committee's activities.

In every case the committee should study the documents sent in by applicants or by people nominating candidates. These constitute the basic dossier for each candidate. For some the information will be skimpy. Should the committee seek more biographical information? Should it check references? Should it engage in telephone conversations with candidates? Should it hold preliminary interviews with any?

Some boards of trustees are quite clear on what the committee should not do. For example, some boards prohibit the screening committee from writing to or telephoning references or communicating directly with candidates, stipulating that such inquiries should be left to the selection committee. Most boards, however, are quite prepared to have the committee seek the necessary biographical data and collect judgments about the candidates. Indeed, it is difficult to see how committees can do an adequate job of screening unless they seek fairly complete information on each candidate.

All public notices calling attention to the vacancy should request respondents to send their *curricula vitae* along with their application. If they fail to send sufficient information, the committee's staff member or secretary should request whatever is needed.

In the case of nominees the situation is a little more delicate. Some will not be worth much of the committee's time; some will never be interested; some will; and some may become interested if approached in the right way. To write and ask whether interested and, if so, to send biographical material is to risk losing at the very start those who ultimately may become most attractive. If the nominator has not sent in sufficient information, the committee can ask for more, can check the standard reference sources, and can make inquiries of third parties who are presumed to know the individual.[2] Often the nominee is not aware that he or she has been nominated. In some cases, of course, the nominees know that they have been nominated, and there is no reason not to communicate directly with them. Exhibits I, J, K, L, and M give five sample letters used by a liberal arts college to seek more information and to thank those who took the trouble to respond.

How should the biographical data be presented to the committee? Some committees—more in the public sector than in the private—insist that all candidates fill out a standard form. This has the merit of providing comparable data on all candidates and thereby of making comparisons among candidates much easier, but it is likely to be a barrier to the reluctant or sophisticated candidate. Other committees prefer to leave the presentation of personal information to the individual, believing that they learn something about that individual by the way

in which he or she writes the information.[3]

A compromise between the two methods used by some committees is to allow candidates to present their data in their own way, and then the secretary or staff member to the committee summarizes the salient points on a standard form, which can serve as a cover to the *curriculum vitae*. This may prove to be more work than is really necessary, as each committee member will want to make his or her own notes on the candidates' material.

References—How Much Value?

Letters of reference are a standard procedure in almost all personnel situations.

Letters attached to the application are of very little value. Written for the eyes of the applicant as well as those of the prospective employer, they are unlikely to present an objective appraisal of strengths and weaknesses. References with whom the committee gets in touch can occasionally be quite informative, but they also suffer from being written by friends of the candidate. It was the judgment of many of our respondents that they have minimal value. "I am now more keenly aware than ever," wrote the board chairman of one small college, "that letters of recommendation are nothing more than perfunctory. The preselection of persons for recommendations on the part of candidates makes them totally of no impact."[4]

Nevertheless, any committee would be faulted which failed to check out the judgment of others who know the candidate. What can be done to make such references of greater value? One way is to seek references not supplied by the individual under consideration. This can be done by asking references so supplied for the names of others who can inform the committee about the candidate, or by making use of contacts committee members have with other institutions or in other localities to ferret out people who know and will comment on the candidate. Great care must be taken not to embarrass the candidate or potential candidate, as noted at the end of this section.

This last gambit can be done more easily and quickly by telephone than by letter, and that brings us to a second way of enhancing the value of references—the telephone. It is convenient to have comments in writing, which become part of the candidate's dossier and which can easily be copied for the benefit of committee members, but this is of little value if the letters say nothing of significance. Conversations on the telephone can be much more revealing. People will say more than they will write. They respond to specific questions. Their inflections and hesitations in expressing their views can sometimes be more revealing than their actual words.

Checking out candidates by telephone can become a problem to the committee if the strategy is not carefully planned in advance. Individual committee members should not take off on their own, calling upon friends on other campuses. This can be disastrous. The division of labor in screening candidates needs to be established and approved in advance, so that the committee's time is spent discussing what is learned rather than wasted in bickering over the authority of a committee member to make the inquiry. One way to avoid trouble is to authorize one member, perhaps the chairperson, to make the calls. Since, however, people respond more honestly to friends and acquaintances, there are some advantages in capitalizing on personal connections.

What is needed is agreement on what should be asked. Some committees prefer a standard format or set of questions, and certainly telephone conversations should be shaped by an agreed upon framework. Different candidates, however, raise different questions in the minds of committee members. It is not only appropriate, but desirable to ask whether X really has the strength to stand up to unpopular decisions and whether Y is genuinely concerned about academic issues. Checking references by telephone requires considerable skill—more skill than some committee members are likely to have. An experienced consultant can be of real help at this point.

In writing or telephoning references one caution must constantly be kept in mind, at least in those situations where confidentiality is important. It is not a problem in open selection procedures. If the individual does not want his or her candidacy publicly known, especially in the present place of employment (and the committee must honor this request), references must not be sought from people where the inquiry would embarrass the candidate. Where it is appropriate to proceed, the inquirer should request that his or her informant respect the confidential nature of the inquiry. Where the individual is not yet a candidate, this fact must be made clear in any communication with a third party.

Preliminary Interviews?

How soon should committees start interviewing candidates? As we have noted, some committees are expressly instructed not to make direct contact with candidates. The conventional procedure is to postpone interviews until the screening process has reduced the roster to the select list.

There are two reasons for questioning the soundness of the conventional view. Some committees reported that a few early interviews with apparently strong candidates were highly educational to the committee. Such interviews enabled them to focus more clearly on what it was they were looking for and to appraise more realistically the paper credentials of the candidates.

Second, the opportunity to get acquainted and to exchange ideas afforded by the interview can make a critical difference in developing an interest or maintaining an interest on the part of the candidate in a given situation. Remember that some candidates need to be persuaded to consider the job. Communication at a distance punctuated by intervals of silence is less likely to generate interest than personal contact. Conversely, the interest aroused by an early interview is likely to be dissipated by long delays. Interviews should not normally take place until the end of the search process is in sight.

Rating Systems

The end product of the screening process is the select list. During the weeks or months spent in this screening exercise candidates are sorted into different groups. Fairly standard classifications are (1) prime candidates, (2) possibly worth further consideration, (3)

not qualified, and (4) deferred for further information. Some committees will set aside for special consideration inside candidates. Committees operating under sunshine laws may find it expedient to be more diplomatic in the statement of their ratings than committees that meet in private.

Some committees develop elaborate rating schedules or forms with weighted values for different features of the candidates' qualifications, professional and personal. At their worst, these methods tend to make ratings rather mechanical; at their best, they facilitate compromise and compensate for individual aberrations of judgment. The advice of John A. Dunn, Jr., Associate Vice President of Tufts University and staff officer for their 1976 search committee, is worth considering. "Avoid complex candidate rating systems; the good candidates will surface. Getting through 400 or so candidates is a major job. We formed three 'teams' and rated candidates numerically 1-2-3-4. The top 30 or 40 surfaced on everyone's list."[5]

The ranking or grouping of candidates is a more or less continuous process from the first reading of early applications to final agreement on the select list. In efforts to speed up the process committees will sometimes make snap judgments and end up shortchanging themselves. Committees should be careful, however, not to rank candidates until all the evidence, including interviews, is in. The issue is not merely that candidates deserve thoughtful consideration—after all, their future careers are involved—but also that the standards and insights of committee members change as they progress.

Frederick Bolman in *How College Presidents are Chosen* quotes a dean's statement calculated to make all of us think twice. "The man whom we finally selected as president started out as a little-known name near the bottom of our secondary list. Because of repeated references by outsiders, his name began to work its way upward on the secondary list until finally it was at the top. Then it was placed at the bottom of our 'number one' list. He continued to get extraordinarily glowing recommendations. As a result, his name continued to move up. Finally, he and one other man were invited to the campus for an interview. In the end, he was elected."

Two Cautions

First, keep constantly in touch with candidates. Keep them informed of their status. They should not be left in the dark. As one president said in criticism of the process by which he was selected: "The length of time in evaluating candidates was too great. There were long periods without any indication from the selection committee of their progress. Stated deadlines for providing information were not met."

Some committees write polite "reject" letters as soon as candidates are rated below the "well qualified" or "possibly qualified" rankings. Others prefer to keep all candidacies alive until the end. Either way, the committee owes it to the candidates and to its own ultimate success to keep in communication with candidates and to give them some notion of where they stand.

Second, as pointed out in Chapter 2, be sure to make records of all oral communications with candidates and with references, and of all committee decisions. With hundreds of candidates confusion is easy, and over months of sorting and sifting memories grow dim. At some future date the committee may have to justify its decisions. When that time comes, full documentation becomes important.

Checklist #5
Screening Candidates

1. What size should the "select list" be? This decision should be included in the trustees' charge to the committee.

2. Who will do the actual screening of candidates?

   a. The whole committee?

   b. One or more teams of committee members?

   c. Advisory committee(s) of faculty and/or staff and students?

   d. The chairperson or staff person or some one committee member?

   e. An outside consultant?

3. How extensive an investigation should the committee make?

   a. Should the committee limit itself to information provided by the applicants and nominators?

   b. How to acquire additional biographical data: by correspondence with applicants and nominators; by research in public reference books; through the candidates' references; through individuals not designated by candidates?

4. To use or not to use the telephone?
   a. By whom?
   b. On an individual basis or with standard set questions?

5. Should the committee hold early interviews with promising candidates?

6. What kind of rating system?

---

1. The committee report for one eastern state university contains the following passage: "By mid-November, a substantial number of candidates' qualifications had been received. The committee directed the secretary to screen initially all folders to (a) identify those applicants who were obviously ill-suited for the position, (b) identify those candidates who had extraordinarily fine credentials, and (c) identify those candidates who appeared to have at least the minimum qualifications and who would require further study."

2. This is brought home by the following passage from the committee report of an eastern private university: "Involved in the presentation to members of *equal* data on all candidates is a full-time research effort in public sources for biographical materials. A part of this may involve telephone contacts to seek additional information. For this committee, such research was intensive for a six-week period, and adequate staff should be provided to complete the work. If the committee chooses, as did the present group, not to inform nominees of their involvement by prior contact for information, this research phase is of special importance."

3. For those who are interested in the arguments pro and con, *see* the article "Selecting Academic Administrators" by Thomas M. Stauffer in *Educational Record*, vol. 57, no. 3, September 1976, and the commentary on the article by Frederick S. Weaver and Louise T. Farnham in vol. 58, no. 3 of the same journal.

4. A perceptive observer commented on giving references: "I'm always concerned about the quality of the recommendations, even their truthfulness. The difficulty is getting the 'whole truth.' It's one thing for me to say that so-and-so is a fine person. If I am obliged to rate them on a scale as compared to others I have known, I may be forced to be more specific and that is an advantage to the interviewer."

5. Panel discussion at AGB National Conference on Trusteeship, Williamsburg, Virginia, March 1977.

Chapter 6

Step Six—
Interviewing Candidates

S creening candidates, chiefly on the basis of their written credentials, is the first step in sorting through the pool. Interviewing those who have survived is the second. This is an essential operation. No committee that knows its business will nominate candidates for the presidency of the institution without having seen and talked with them face-to-face; and no board worth its salt will appoint anyone sight unseen.[1]

A Risky Business

Interviews are essential; they are also difficult and must be handled with skill. Firsthand impressions can be very misleading. Some candidates may turn on the charm and dazzle the committee with a brilliant but misleading performance. Other candidates will be reticent, either by temperament or because they prefer to conceal some part of their past. It takes a skilled interrogator to draw them out.

Interviewing is a fine art that not everyone possesses. One perceptive administrator who served as chief staff member to a university selection committee writes: "I have some sense that committees can get into more trouble in the interviewing stage than in the screening stage. We tried to avoid this by asking our director of personnel to conduct a briefing session for the interviewing committees on how to interview. Everyone (especially successful people like trustees) thinks he is a good interviewer. And very few are."

All committees would do well to think hard about the process of interviewing, and most members could profit from a little professional guidance. A training session or a practice run under the expert supervision of a consultant will greatly improve the performance of interviewing teams. All this is important because the results of the interviews are often so decisive.

When asked what kind of evidence about candidates had been most persuasive, the dominant answer from committee members was the interview. Not only was it "the most fruitful part of the process," to quote one board chairman, it also led to dramatic changes in comparative rankings. "We continued to be surprised," wrote another chairman, "by the magnitude of the discrepancies that existed between images formed on the basis of applications and recommendations and images generated on the basis of direct contact with candidates."

Not everyone, however, will rate interviews as highly as did the majority of our respondents. Donald Fouts, for example, in the article "Picking a President the Business Way" already referred to, argues that the appraisal of candidates should be based primarily on "rigorous, independent investigation," which goes to the people who know the candidates well and have observed them in actual operation. In his judgment, the interview should come later and concentrate on considerations of personality, poise, and similar qualities amenable to evaluation via an interview. "It is important to note," Fouts concludes, "that utilizing the interview as a secondary source of data in no way denigrates its role in the selection process. Indeed, the interview performance may appropriately be used as the determining factor in the final selection. The only caveat is that the interview should not take the place of independent investigation or be scheduled before independent investigation has been completed."[2]

This is a tenable, but in our opinion undesirable, position. Most committees use the interview as a means to arrive at the select list by screening out candidates who have survived the first and second rounds. The final check on competence and suitability through communication with those intimately acquainted with the candidates' work and personality and track record should follow the interview.

A Two-Way Street

The interview is usually the first face-to-face contact between the candidate and members of the committee—sometimes after weeks or months of correspondence and waiting. The impressions gained on both sides are often crucial. Committees must remember that the candidate is judging the college or university just as the committee is appraising the candidate.

The best candidates, as we have noted, are often reluctant candidates who need to be courted. They will be influenced by the way they are treated, the kind of questions asked, the degree of consideration for their inquiries, the setting and atmosphere of the interview, the amount of knowledge about and enthusiasm for the college or university on the part of trustees. Committee members have the difficult role of both interrogators and salesmen.[3]

Thoughtful candidates will come to the interview full of questions about the way the institution operates and about its problems and prospects. They will also be curious about the extent to which trustees, faculty, and others understand those problems and prospects and the degree of their commitment to the institution. If the institution is a public college or university, they will want to know about the political climate and the influence of the governor's office, the legislative committee on education, and the budget office. If the institution is part of a multi-campus system, candidates may want to supplement their impressions with first-hand analyses of interinstitutional cooperation or conflict. (See the sample on pages 66 and 67 of Chapter VII for the kind of questions that candidates are likely to have on their minds and that committee members should be prepared to discuss.)

Candidates should have received extensive information about the institution in advance of the interview.[4] A recurrent complaint from the newly elected presidents in our survey, especially from those at community colleges, was their lack of exposure to the people and problems of the institution before they had to make a decision about the job.

The interview is a golden opportunity to sell the college or university. This is partly a matter of information, partly of atmosphere and attitude. Interviews are not always easy for candidates whose careers are at stake. Their reaction to the institution will depend in part on their impressions of the people with whom they are dealing. Thus, the manner in which the interviews are conducted is very important. Here the chairperson plays a decisive role, for he or she is responsible for putting the candidate at ease, for directing the course of the inquisition, for curbing irrelevancies, for stopping the undiplomatic committee member, and for easing an embarrassing situation by humor or a change of topic.

Committees sometimes resent inquiries by candidates, whereas they should welcome them. More often the failure to provide full information to the candidate is accidental. Full disclosure and complete candor are very important.

How Many Interviews?

In our survey the number of candidates interviewed ranged from one to thirty—with more in the 20 to 30 range than one would have expected and with no significant differences between public and private, four-year and two-year, institutions. Our survey did not provide enough figures for significant averages or medians, but it would appear that most committees interview between five and fifteen candidates in the first round.

The number will be determined in part by the nature and extent of the screening process. One private college that interviewed thirty candidates concluded in its review of the selection process that a few well-placed telephone calls would have enabled it to cut the number of interviews in half.

The temptation is to skimp on interviews for reasons of cost, the amount of time and energy required of committee members, and the danger of raising false expectations on the part of candidates. The first argument is wrong. We can only reiterate that the choice of the next president justifies whatever investment of money may be required. Committee time is not unlimited, but as with money the importance of the job justifies whatever output is necessary. Interviews do raise hopes and may be misinterpreted by candidates and their friends. This is a risk, but a far less serious one than overlooking the right individual on the basis of written credentials. Where doubts or differences of opinion exist in the minds of the committee members, it becomes all the more important to see the candidates.

Scheduling Interviews

There is no standard rule about where interviews should take place. Some institutions send teams to interview candidates on their home ground. This is often more revealing than interviews elsewhere, but it is potentially more embarrassing to the candidates. This practice should, therefore, be employed with great caution and should not be used in the first round of interviews.

Private colleges and universities, where concern for maintaining confidentiality is high, tend to select neutral sites, either an off-campus hotel or motel, a trustee's office, or a major transportation center such as Chicago, New York, or Atlanta where candidates and committee members can conveniently gather.

Public institutions and especially community colleges are more inclined to hold interviews on campus. For many of them confidentiality is less important than convenience, and in some states everything is out in the open.

Wherever held, the physical setting of the interviews should be pleasant. Candidates' expenses should be covered. It is not customary to include spouses at the first interview; but if they are invited, their expenses should also be paid. Arrangements

should be made for overnight accomodations, if necessary. Some thought needs to be given to the kind of room in which the interviews take place and to the placing of chairs and tables to create an informal and, so far as possible, a relaxed atmosphere. If candidates are to be kept waiting, a pleasant place to wait is important.

Interviews should not be rushed. To save time it is tempting to crowd them close together. One-hour interviews are apt to be perfunctory. Most committees find that they want two to three hours for each individual. On this kind of schedule three (or at most, four) interviews are enough for one day. Interviewing is hard work, and after several hours one inevitbly grows weary. Some break between interviews will give committee members a chance to compare impressions and to make notes.[5]

Some interviews may turn out to be a waste of time. Out of courtesy to the candidates, however, they should not be cut short. The schedule of interviews should be so arranged that candidates do not fall over one another. Even where the select list is public knowledge, candidates should be kept out of each other's way. On one private college campus candidates were whisked about from one faculty house to another to prevent them from meeting. In another situation all candidates were invited to the campus the same day, repeatedly bumped into each other, and reported that they found the process "demeaning and degrading." The president of a community college reported: "In my particular situation, several candidates were brought together at the same time for purposes of interviewing and social interaction (the search committee did conduct individual interviews). I personally found this to be a most clumsy and confusing manner in which to conduct the search. I would have preferred more emphasis on individual treatment."

The Interviewing Team

Who should do the interviewing? The whole committee if possible, and this is an argument for holding the interviews on or near the campus. For reasons of convenience and expense many committees set up one or more teams of interviewers. It may be a single subcommittee composed of a trustee, faculty member, and student, or the committee may divide into two or more teams. The latter runs the risk that members of one team will react to candidates differently from the members of another team. This could lead to the elimination of an individual whom the committee as a whole might have kept in the running.

If it can be managed, it is better to have the entire committee involved in each interview. This makes it easier to reach consensus. It makes a good impression on candidates. It permits each constituency represented on the committee to get answers to its concerns. It avoids the danger of subteams becoming advocates for "their" candidates. Interviews should not be obviously "staged," though they should be well planned in advance. The chairperson who naturally introduces the questioning should not take over but allow others a full opportunity to pose questions.

A wise principle is not to eliminate any candidate about whom there is a serious difference of opinion and certainly not to do so

unless more than one member of the committee is strongly opposed to the candidate. Since, however, all candidates favored by a subcommittee will be reviewed by the committee as a whole (and quite possibly interviewed by the whole committee), the danger of a too favorable judgment by one team will be avoided.

Interviews by single committee members should be avoided so far as possible. This is sometimes specifically outlawed by the ground rules under which the committee operates. Occasionally, a committee member will find himself or herself in the vicinity of a candidate and may be encouraged by other members to seize the opportunity for information at first hand. This can be helpful, but should only be done with the knowledge and approval of the committee. It should not be used as a substitute for an interview by the whole committee or by one of its teams.

A few committees in our survey relied on professional consultants to conduct preliminary interviews. As noted in Chapter 2, the outside consultant has certain advantages in talking with candidates. As a professional personnel officer, the consultant brings the special skills important to good interviewing. As a person of wide experience in the educational field, he or she is better prepared than the average committee member to relate personality traits to institutional needs and problems. As a third party outside the immediate family, the consultant is in a strategic position to interpret the institution's situation and opportunities to the candidate in more realistic and persuasive terms than can most committee members, and for the same reason can more easily and gracefully find out how genuinely interested the candidate is.

What Questions To Ask?

Committee members should know a great deal about the candidate by the time he or she comes for an interview, and the members should have the full biographical record— age, education, family, professional positions, public statements on educational issues, and the like — freshly in mind at the time of the interview.

The great merit of the interview is the impression it provides of personality, character, style. What kind of a person is this? How comprehensive is his or her understanding, how sharp the edge of the mind, how quick the forensic skill? Has the candidate a sense of humor and a sense of compassion?

The interview also can throw some light on unresolved questions in the minds of committee members. The candidate's positions with regard to research, teaching, tenure, collective bargaining, graduate study, professional programs, institutional governance can be explored. Ambiguous or contradictory comments from references about the candidate can be pursued and assessed.

Should candidates be asked a standard set of questions or should each interview be custom-tailored? As indicated in the preceding paragraph, each individual record will have its own blank spots or ambiguous areas that need clearing up. This argues for tailoring the interviews to the individuals. The art of interviewing involves thinking about each interviewee in advance and designing the kind of interrogation that will exhibit the strengths and weaknesses, the

professional competence, and the human qualities of the candidate.[6]

However important, this kind of questioning makes comparisons difficult. Since comparative judgments are the nature of the exercise, committees find themselves pushed in the direction of a uniform set of questions for all candidates and a rating sheet or form on which to score the answers. These can sometimes become quite detailed and mechanical. Open-ended questions tend to be more illuminating. Exhibits N and O provide two examples: a quite simple set used by a midwestern liberal arts college and an excerpt from a much more elaborate formula of another institution. Further suggestions can be found in Herbert Hengst's article, "Interviewing the Candidate for President" in *AGB Reports*, vol. 20, no. 1, January/February 1978.

Committee members should keep in mind federal and state restrictions on asking certain kinds of questions. State regulations vary.[7]

Tying Up the Results

Certain actions should follow immediately upon the interviews.

1. Committee members should record their individual impressions. Whether this is done on some previously agreed upon rating sheet or in the form of scribbled notes, reactions to the strengths and weaknesses of the candidates interviewed should be promptly recorded. With a dozen personalities being compared, it is easy to become forgetful or uncertain. The written record becomes invaluable.

2. The select list (candidates judged worth

interviewing) should become even more select (candidates judged worth inviting to meet with board members or to the campus for wide exposure). How to handle those candidates who survive the interviews is the subject of the next chapter. The committee's decision about the survivors should follow on the heels of the last interview.

3. Once the decisions about finalists have been made, the chairperson or the committee's administrative officer on behalf of the chairperson should promptly get in touch with the candidates, advising them of their status. If the committee's preliminary decision is still favorable, tell the candidate so—

and use the occasion to make certain that the candidate is still actively interested. If the committee is not interested, the candidate should be so informed.[8] If a decision must wait upon the completion of other interviews or more information, tell the candidate that he or she will be hearing from the committee within such and such a time. There is nothing so demoralizing to the candidate as to be left dangling after the interview. Exhibit P presents a typical "reject" letter.

At this stage the search for the new president is approaching its climax. Keep in communication.

Additional Sources of Information

Warren G. Bennis: *The Leaning Ivory Tower*, Jossey-Bass Publishers 1973. Chapter 2, "Searching for the 'Perfect' President" is an amusing account of the search process as seen by the candidate. A catastrophic interview is described on pages 30-31.

Frederick deW. Bolman: *How College Presidents are Chosen*, American Council on Education 1965.

Joseph F. Kauffman: *The Selection of College and University Presidents*, Association of American Colleges 1974.

Richard A. Kaplowitz: *Selecting Academic Administrators: The Search Committee*, American Council

on Educaton 1973. Donald E. Fouts: "Picking a President the Business Way," *AGB Reports*, vol. 19, no. 1, January/February 1977.

Frank R. Miller: *The Selection and Appointment of School Heads*, National Association of Independent Schools 1975. While aimed primarily at private secondary schools, the problems are much the same, and the discussion of interviews with candidates is very good.

Herbert R. Hengst: "Interviewing the Candidate for President" *AGB Reports*, vol. 20, no. 1, January/February 1978.

Checklist #6
Interviewing Candidates

1. The committee should decide:

   a. How to make interviews effective.

   b. How many candidates to interview.

   c. Where to hold interviews:
      (1) on campus,
      (2) neutral site.

   d. On convenient and comfortable physical arrangements.

   e. On schedule of interviews.

   f. What questions to ask.

   g. Who should do the interviewing:
      (1) the entire committee,
      (2) one or more teams,
      (3) professional consultants.

   h. What information to provide candidates.

   i. How much effort to sell the candidates.

2. At end of interviews committee should:

   a. Reduce the list of candidates.

   b. Decide on next steps.

   c. Inform candidates of their status.

---

1. One midwestern university committee chairperson reported in our survey that no trustee attended any of the scheduled interviews for their six finalists, which may account for the fact that the board did not appoint the candidate whom the committee recommended most strongly. And the president of an eastern college noted that, "the chairman of the board did not meet me personally until *after* I was elected." These are the aberrations which cause dismay.

2. *AGB Reports*, vol. 19, no. 1., January/February 1977, p. 10.

3. Consider the perceptive comment of Professors Frederick S. Weaver and Louise T. Farnham: "Faculty and student committee members are interviewing their future supervisor or someone who will have a direct effect on their work. Relevant information should be gathered with as much discretion and taste as humanly possible, for reasons of future working relationships as well as in the interests of finding and hiring the best possible candidate." "On Selecting Academic Administrators" in the *Educational Record*, vol. 58, no. 3, September 1977, p. 324.

4. The committee at one state university prepared a slide presentation on the university which, together with a 16 mm. film produced by the local Chamber of Commerce, was shown to each candidate in connection with the interview.

5. The committee of one liberal arts college divided into two halves for the interviews. Each candidate met with each half-committee. This had the advantage of reducing the size of the interviewing group, which made it less formidable to the candidates, of giving the candidates the opportunity of correcting a poor performance with one group by a better performance with the other, and of allowing the two halves to compare notes at the end of the day.

6. Some questions should not be asked. Consult university counsel or its affirmative action officer.

7. In New York, for example, the Division of Human Rights, Ruling on Inquiries #26,050, November 1979 declares unlawful questions regarding potential employees' race, color, religion, national origin, sex, marital status, and arrest record.

8. One correspondent speaking from personal experience calls attention to a special situation. "A committee may sometimes leave a name on the list for some political or sentimental reason when it is clear to the committee that that person is not going to be chosen. But this is a mistake: postponing the removal of a name simply makes for trouble, not courtesy; it builds false hopes either in the candidate or in partisans."

Chapter 7

Step Seven—
Selecting
Top Candidates

After the interviews with candidates, the real soul-searching begins. Occasionally committee members will be so unanimous in their preference, so convinced that they have identified just the right person to be the next president, that they are prepared to make a recommendation to the trustees without further ado—without, that is, further checking into past performance and without further involvement of faculty, administrative staff, or students. Attractive, however, as it may seem to bypass several steps in the laborious process of selection, this is a risky procedure. Sudden attraction is not always the best augury for permanent marriage.

Normally, the committee should be able to reduce its roster of candidates after interviews to eight and preferably to five, depending on the number interviewed, each of whom looks promising. At this point most committees face two assignments. The first is to complete the investigation of the candidates (unless, following Fouts—see page 52—that has already been done), to get as much information as possible on their background and performance. The second is to expose them and the college or university community to each other in order to find out how compatible and enthusiastic they are after closer acquaintance and inspection. In a sense, the campus visit is one more step in checking out the candidate. Usually it is the last one.

As the search narrows, it becomes more intense. Sometimes committees will want second interviews with certain candidates to fill in gaps or to settle differences of opinion.

Rigorous Background Check

The normal procedure at this point is to make a thorough investigation of the background and professional performance of the individuals who are potential candidates for campus visits. This kind of investigation, the importance of which can hardly be overstated, can be made during the earlier screening process. Some commentators, like Fouts, recommend that it precede interviews; but, in view of the potential embarrassment resulting from local investigations (unless done with professional skill), it is better to hold off until the list of candidates has been reduced to the finalists. Some candidates will strongly prefer that this kind of home-base investigation be deferred until after they have visited the campus that is seeking a president.

There comes a time, however, when local inquiries cannot be postponed any longer. They can and should be made with sensitivity and with the knowledge and permission of the candidates. If at this stage the candidate is still reluctant to have inquiries made on his own campus, the committee would be well advised to scratch his or her name. The failure to investigate thoroughly can be a fatal mistake. "We didn't visit all candidates on their own campuses. This would be helpful," wrote the board chairperson of a private junior college in response to our question about how she would proceed differently if it all had to be done over again. Another would institute on-site visits, which had been omitted altogether.

Presumably during the screening process committees will have been in communication with the references supplied by the candidates. These, being preselected, are likely to have limited value. It is important to be in touch with others who have worked closely with the candidate both in his or her present position and in previous positions and who can give independent appraisals of their personality, capacity to work well with others, to delegate responsibility, to function under stress, to exemplify in private as well as public life the qualities for which the committee is looking. This is the sort of assessment the committee needs at this stage. It should be a composite assessment, for no one sees the whole individual. Those for whom the candidate has worked may have a quite different picture from those who have worked for the candidate. Performance in one job may differ markedly from performance in another. The hostile critic needs to be discounted as much as the undiscriminating friend.

Background information of this kind can be obtained by correspondence, by telephone calls, and by personal visits. While there are some advantages in having an evaluation in writing, most individuals tend to be less frank and less detailed in writing than in conversation. At this late stage letters also cause too much delay.

Telephone calls are less expensive and, except for the person who telephones, less time-consuming than on-site visits. Whether they are less satisfactory as well is a moot point. Some people communicate better face-to-face. The visual and personal relation is likely to improve both the quality and the quantity of communication. People tend to speak more freely and fully than they write. Their inflections and hesitations can reveal information not to be found in a written statement.

The candidate should know that an investigation is underway. Inquiries, whether made by a designated committee member or by a team of members, might well begin with individuals suggested by the candidate, but it should be understood by the candidate that they will not stop there.

Some faculty members and administrators who are presidential candidates and who are employed by public institutions, even in states where there are no sunshine laws, have no objection to having their candidacy known. For them on-site visits of inquiry constitute no problem. But, even where every effort is made to maintain confidentiality, as in most private institutional searches, word leaks out; and some, if not all, of a candidate's colleagues are likely to know that he or she is an active candidate. Those making the investigation still are responsible for safeguarding the candidate and can do so by taking the line: "So-and-so has been suggested to us as a suitable person to be president of X University. We would like your judgment." This approach is especially important in those cases where there have been no leaks. The resulting conversation should reveal much that the committee wants to know.

Background investigations can be pursued in a variety of ways. The people queried and the questions asked may well differ for public and private institutions. Here is one example of how the chairman of a well-organized private university search went about it: "I personally called all the references for the six candidates and made a report on the telephone conversations, which was sent to every member of the committee. These calls followed the format generated by the following list of questions:

"A. Was there anything in his background that could turn up later that could embarrass us personally?

"B. Would he and his family fit into the small college, small town situation?

"C. His leadership ability.

"D. His stage presence.

"E. Does he wear well?

"F. His energy.

"G. His commitment.

"H. Can you work for him?

"I. Would you work for him?

"J. Is there anything we should know that I didn't ask?"

The procedure of the committee at another institution was described as follows: "Just in advance of campus visits, one final inquiry was made in order to be as thorough as possible in investigating the qualifications of the finalists. Believing that there is certain information one cannot learn from dossiers, interviews or references, teams from Denison, with the candidate's permission, visited each finalist's home campus to talk with students, faculty, administrators and trustees about the candidate's performance in his current environment. Such exhaustive investigations are rarely made in college searches, but the information obtained in these visits proved well worth the effort."[1]

Here again an outside professional consultant can be very useful. With a broad background of information and trained in the technique of investigation, the professional knows what questions to ask, where the answers can be found, and how to evaluate conflicting responses. He or she can move about the campus and community in less conspicuous fashion and will therefore cause less local excitement. Furthermore, the consultant need not reveal (if there is reason for keeping it secret) the institution on whose behalf he or she is making inquiries.

The Campus Visit— Pluses and Minuses

Having winnowed its original roster of candidates by screening based on credentials, interviews, and investigations of past performance, the committee must now decide which candidates should be invited for campus visits.

A few of our presidential respondents reported that they were offered — and accepted—the presidency without ever having visited the institution. Presumably, they were already sufficiently familiar with the local scene to make a visit unnecessary or so desperate to leave their current jobs that they were quite prepared to leap into the unknown (not a good augury for success).

Earl W. Porter, Secretary of the University of Illinois and Secretary for the board of trustees, was involved in a recent survey of the selection process for presidents of large, complex state universities, whether multicampus or organized as a statewide system. He found widespread reluctance among the top officers of these institutions to show up as a candidate on another cam-

pus. Said Porter: "As a group, they are likely to be familiar with most of the universities that approach them, will have visited them from time to time, may know some of the staff, and have a general idea of the resources and influences. In short, they are in the club and their questions are more subtle. If they need information, it will be to update what they already know, to sound out the present situation on the board of trustees, to know the circumstances under which the incumbent is leaving. If they wish, they can inquire about these and other matters indirectly and quietly. A final public visit, during which they may be recognized, may be risky and of minimal value."[2]

Most candidates, however, will want to have their own look at the inviting institution. Unless they are already familiar with it, they will want to see what the campus is like—buildings, grounds, and location. They will want to get some measure of the faculty's concern for educational issues, the composition and quality of the student body, the structure and competence of the administrative staff. They will want to talk with administrative officers with whom they would be working. They will want to see the outgoing president to get his or her assessment of future prospects. What they find may turn them off; or, hesitant and skeptical before the visit, they may find themselves turned on.

At the same time the various constituencies on campus will be eager to see what the candidates look like, what impression they make, whether they are educators or managers, scholars or fund raisers, how they stand on fraternities and similar issues. These constituencies would like to feel that they had some voice in the final selection. And because it is important that the new president at least start with the good will of these constituencies, there is considerable pressure on committees to put their final candidates on public view.

Faculty members will sometimes resent what they see as a deliberate indifference to their concerns and their judgment if they are not allowed a preview and will occasionally react with virulent hostility to the person appointed. Several colleges and universities have faced the painful situation of a faculty demanding that the trustees withdraw their offer.

Yet there are clear and present dangers in public campus visits. The most obvious is that the candidate's cover will be blown. This need not happen. Private colleges and smaller state institutions have succeeded with careful planning in exposing candidates to a wide variety of local constituents without generating a burst of publicity; but, this requires a high degree of cooperation and discipline on the part of the members of the college community. Committees can minimize the danger of a breach of confidentiality; they cannot guarantee that damage will not occur.

A second danger is that the appearance of several candidates on campus turns the selection into a pseudo-popularity contest. Candidates are paraded in front of various groups for approval. A candidate's performance might be so outrageous or intolerable that his or her candidacy would come to an abrupt end. But the superficial impressions gleaned from brief appearances are inadequate as

the basis for preferring one candidate over another.

A third danger lies in the invitation to dirty politics. Subtle, and sometimes not so subtle, campaigns can be carried on in favor of one candidate rather than another. Supporters of an inside candidate can leak the names of outsiders to the press, with the result that the outside candidates will feel forced to withdraw. This is no way in which to conduct an intelligent search and selection.

Finally, many candidates will take umbrage at the very notion of putting on a song-and-dance act for the benefit of faculty or students. The whole concept is offensive to them. They are prepared to be judged *in camera* by a selection committee or by the board as a whole where their merits or defects can be carefully weighed. They are not interested in a Roman Circus where their fate is decided by the mood of the audience.

Where does this leave us? We have pointed out before and emphasize it once again that presidents, no matter how outstanding, must live with faculty, students, administrative officers, alumni, state education officials, and others. To be effective, they must have the support of whichever groups are most powerful, and the best way of ensuring the support of those groups at the start is by involving them in the selection. Practically, the best way of doing this is to have the key constituencies represented on the search and selection committee or committees and to have those committees maintain rapport with their constituencies. This is not only a legitimate delegation of authority; it is an essential one. As has been said before, the committee will have studied the candidates' records for weeks and months. Committee members are in the best position to make intelligent recommendations.

Each search and selection committee, however, will have to decide for itself whether to keep candidates under wraps until the appointment has been made or whether to display them before campus groups. Where premature disclosure is not a problem, one important barrier to campus visits is removed. Where candidates are eager to meet with faculty and students, they should be accommodated. Traditional practices and the temper of the campus may suggest one procedure rather than another.

Candidates on Parade

Let us assume that the decision has been made in favor of public appearance. Whether several candidates or only the committee's top choice are invited, plans need to be made with great care.

One-day visits are barely adequate. A day and a half to two full days are much better. One state university arranged visits of four days each for its four finalists.[3] And the campus should concentrate on one candidate at a time, not only to avoid the embarrassment of candidates bumping into one another, but also to extract as much advantage as possible by focusing on one individual.

Decisions must be made about who will meet the candidate and under what circumstances—all the faculty members who are interested or selected representatives of divergent faculty groups, students at large or members of the student government association, which administrative officers, which representatives of the denomination with which the institution is related (if any), local alumni, community leaders, state educational officers (if public), trustees other than those on the selection committee.

With so many people eager to get into the act, the candidate's schedule must be carefully planned well in advance. The board and committee chairman of a church-related college in the south described their program as follows: "When we brought a candidate to the community for an interview, we always requested that the candidate bring his wife. We planned a very comprehensive schedule of interviews for these candidates, which included a meeting with all department heads on the faculty, a meeting with student leaders, a meeting with some trustees, and, of course, meetings with members of the search committee. These meetings were normally culminated at the end of the second day with a dinner and social hour at my home, followed by a two or three-hour session between the candidate and the members of the search committee. This type of social arrangement also gave our spouses an opportunity to visit with the wife of the applicant. Thus, we obtained input on the adaptability of the candidate's wife to our particular situation."

The chairperson of the southern state university referred to previously described in general terms the four-day visits of the four candidates and their wives who were invited to the campus. "Their schedule was very busy, usually starting about 6:30 a.m. and concluding during the evening. We arranged several interviews and meetings with the major elements of the university, in addition to sessions with the selection committee. Actually, they met with over 100 members of the university. These included the board of trustees, top administrators, deans and department chairpersons, members of the faculty senate and representatives of the student body. The candidates were subjected to a very comprehensive review by our associates on the campus." Exhibit Q presents a typical schedule for visits to the campus.

Some selection committees find an initial meeting with the candidate a useful and gracious introduction to the campus. Other committees prefer to end with such a meeting—to find out what kind of experience the candidate has had, what questions and reactions were generated, what problems remain to be settled.

All this sounds strenuous, and indeed it is—unavoidably so. One wants to be gracious, friendly, relaxed, to create a favorable impression on the candidate. Yet there is so much to be covered in a limited time.

There is, however, a side benefit to setting up a fairly crowded schedule. That is the way the new president will be living his or her professional life, and it may be well to observe the candidate under pressure. In the words of one thoughtful chairman: "Though I am not quite sure of how this would go over with super professionals, I am convinced that some index of the candidate's reaction to pressure would be most helpful. Such an examination would not ensure but might preclude the institution being involved in the 'Peter Principle' [promoting persons to their levels of administrative incompetency]."

Faculty and student members of the committee, or faculty and student advisory committees as the case may be, can take major responsibility for much of the candidate's visit; but, each candidate should have one member of the committee or one administrative officer as his or her specific host, whose responsibility it would be to shepherd the candidate from interview to interview, to introduce and to explain, to make special arrangements when necessary and to alter the schedule if desired. The host should meet the candidate at the airport or wherever, make certain that overnight accomodations are satisfactory and attractive, see that the candidate gets to appointments on time, and in general stay with the candidate until departure.

At group meetings the host should probably be present—to mediate if necessary, to observe reactions, and to interpret to the candidate afterwards why certain questions were raised and who it was who pushed a certain line of inquiry. At individual conferences with administrative officers, the host's presence is normally not necessary and may interfere with full communication between candidate and staff.[4] Tailored arrangements should be made for the candidate's spouse. These spouses will have special interests and concerns that should be explored. In most instances, they will want to talk with the departing president and spouse. The nature of their concerns is examined in more detail in the section entitled "The President's Spouse."[5]

Educating the Candidates

The campus visit is an opportunity for the candidate to get acquainted with the institution as well as the institution with the candidate. Except for inside candidates it is a vitally important opportunity and one frequently muffed. A sensible and realistic candidate will want to know as much as possible about the institution whose destiny may ultimately be his or her responsibility.

Between 50 and 60 percent of the presidents responded in the affirmative to the question, "Did the search committee provide you with a clear and accurate picture of the opportunities, problems and needs of your institution?" One president of a four-year public university said: "The committee was refreshingly candid." On the other hand, the president of a two-year community college reported: "They were not sure themselves, checked with others in this regard. A couple of board members indicated afterwards that if they indicated how bad things were in their estimate, I might not have taken the job."

Presumably a packet of information about the college or university will be provided all candidates invited to the campus, if not all candidates invited for interviews. Exhibit R contains an example of the kind of material that is useful.

The intelligent candidate will have studied this material in advance and will arrive full of questions about the financial situation, governance structure, temper of faculty and students, public relations of the institution, enrollment trends, collective bargaining (where it exists), and the like. See the following section for the kind of question candidates are likely to ask. Every finalist should be given full opportunity to learn the whole story.[6]

Questions on Candidates' Minds

On finances

Has the institution generated operating surpluses or operating deficits in the last five years?

How much indebtedness? Of what nature?

Has the institution recently experienced any cash-flow difficulties?

What is the condition of the physical plant?

Have there been any developments that would significantly affect the nature of the institution's traditional sources of revenue or the level of support?

For *private institutions*: What is the overall strategy for raising revenue from private sources? When was the last capital campaign? What was the goal and outcome? Is there need for a major fundraising campaign? How has support from private sources changed over the last few years?

For *public institutions*: What has been the recent record of the legislature regarding appropriations to the institution? How do the institution's appropriations, state and federal, compare with appropriations for other institutions in the state?

For *community colleges*: Can local support, in taxes or in donations, be counted on? What are the local problems, if any?

On faculty

Which are the strongest (and the weakest) departments, schools, areas of instruction or research?

What is the rate of faculty turnover? Is there a tenure problem?

Is faculty morale good, bad, or neutral?

Is there a faculty union? Pressure for one? What is the institution's position on unionization?

Have recent accreditation reviews resulted in any recommendations for signficant changes? If so, what kinds of changes were recommended and how have they been dealt with?

On administration

Where is the administration strongest, where the weakest? Are there serious problems in the administrative area?

On students

Has the student body changed in size or composition over the last five years? What is anticipated over the next five?

Is there a dropout problem? How serious?

What percentage of the students are receiving financial aid?

What is the recruitment program?

On the board of trustees

How strong, interested, and active is the board?

What does the board see as its role in governance?

Is there mutual trust among board, faculty, and administration?

Has any legislation, state or federal, been proposed or passed recently that will have a significant effect on the institution?

If a multicampus system, how much authority has the president of each campus?

How much authority resides in the central system office and how much in state offices or with officials such as the budget officer,

the commissioner of education, the governor?

On public relations

Is there a town-gown problem? If so, what has caused it and what can be done about it?

Does the institution have the wholehearted support of its alumni?

For *public institutions*: What kind of liaison does the institution have with the state department of education, the governor's office, the legislature?

For *church-related institutions*: Is the college or university controlled by, supported by, or independent of the parent religious denomination?

In general

What are the major strengths of the institution? Its major weaknesses?

What are the most serious problems needing attention?

What are the three most important contributions a new president could make?

On terms of appointment

What can I expect as compensation?

What are the fringe benefits?

Is there a college or university house in which I must live or am I free to own my own home?

A committee and board that are not able to respond candidly and thoughtfully to questions of this kind are likely to discourage a promising finalist or find themselves later with a surprised and unhappy new president. It is also good practice to provide opportunities for final candidates to meet privately with key officers and faculty members (particularly the chief financial officer). Many of these questions can be explored during these meetings.

The campus visit can also be a glorious opportunity to persuade the candidate of the worth of the institution—the quality of the educational program, the commitment of the faculty, the enthusiasm of the students, the conviction that all problems are surmountable and the future is exciting. Faculty and students need to be alerted to the importance of making the institution attractive to the candidate. All too often they will naively assume that anyone would want to be president of "their" institution. Sometimes with the best of intentions, sometimes with the worst, and often without any thought at all, they can be very rough on candidates. "At the time of my first interview," wrote one new president, "I was turned over to the tender mercies of a hostile faculty group for an entire evening and, as a result, almost withdrew assuming the group was representative. A more balanced faculty group would have been preferable." Amen.

Candidates will be concerned about the terms of their employment. One does not aspire to becoming a college or university president to get rich, but it would be naive to assume that candidates—save in those religious orders where salaries are not paid or not retained—are indifferent to financial considerations.

For the most part candidates are understandably hesitant about making inquiries regarding their remuneration, for fear of seeming to put material considerations ahead of more important matters. Many are prepared to proceed on the formula stated by one president-elect: "A number of things were taken on faith—and that faith was justified." But candidates also might sympathize with the comment of one private college president: "As an inexperienced 'applicant' I regret that I treated terms of appointment rather casually in order not to appear 'pushy.'" A state university president wrote five months after taking office: "At no time have I received a formal (in writing) job offer. Salary and fringe benefits were in doubt until the week I assumed office." Approximately one-third of the new presidents in our survey indicated that the terms of their employment had not been made clear by the time of their official appointment. This is no way to run a railroad!

Sooner or later the terms of employment need to be discussed and the sooner the better. The first interview is the most appropriate time. A subsequent visit to the campus or preliminary meeting with trustees is possible, but risky. If the matter is postponed until time of appointment, the committee and the board risk the withdrawal of the chosen candidate who may find the terms unacceptable. If they delay until a public announcement has been made, they become vulnerable to potentially rough horse trading.[7]

Negotiation over salary and perquisites is not the proper function of the search and selection committee unless it consists entirely of trustees, and even then the subject is better left to the chairperson of the committee or of the board. One or the other, however, should take the initiative in advising the candidates as to what the college or university will probably offer—not necessarily the precise terms, but certainly the range of total compensation contemplated.

The terms themselves are discussed in the following chapter.

The President's Spouse

Time was when college and university presidents were men, save for a sprinkling of Sisters and a few remarkable women. And the men were married to wives whom the trustees assumed would trot along with their husbands in the service of the institution. But times have changed. Slowly but steadily more women are being appointed to top administrative jobs including the presidency; and more and more wives of male presidents have their own professional careers.

The place and role of the male consort can be troublesome, but on the whole it is the lesser problem. There still are fewer of them; and while occasionally a place needs to be found within the faculty or in an administrative position, he usually pursues his own occupation or career outside the institution. Depending on his temperament and interests, he may participate to a greater or less extent in campus social life and extracurricular events. About all that the college or university can ask of him is that he not make demands on his wife's time inconsistent with her obligations and that his personal and professional conduct be above reproach.

On the other hand, the wives of presidents have traditionally been expected to support their husbands' careers. Boards of trustees can no longer take their services for granted—and for free. The fact that many wives today resent being taken for granted and the further fact that more wives are insisting on freedom to continue their professional or outside activities raise in pointed fashion for selection committees and for boards as a whole the question: what are reasonable expectations regarding the wife's place and contribution?

The time to explore these expectations is during the selection process, and since they need to be talked out with the candidate *and spouse*, this means during the interviews or during the campus visits. It is sometimes argued that the college or university is hiring a president, not a spouse, and therefore that the spouse's participation in interviews or campus visits is unnecessary and inappropriate. Many community colleges make few or no demands on the spouse's time and talents, and therefore sometimes do not include him or her in the selection process. But, most college and university boards (and the academic communities as well) do expect the spouse to play a significant role, and in such circumstances it is imperative that he or she be included in interviews and campus visits.[8]

The expectations will vary with the type of institution, its location in a metropolitan or rural setting, and the pattern established by past practice. As noted above, community colleges tend to make fewer demands on the spouse. In small private colleges, the president's wife is normally expected to play an important social role by providing gracious hospitality to trustees, faculty, donors, students and townspeople, by joining her husband in visiting and entertaining alumni, and by participating in campus activities and community organizations. In many large universities, both public and private, the demands can be even heavier. In others the president's spouse is able to keep more aloof from constant daily involvement in university affairs.

Selection committees and board of trustees have generally failed to be as open with both candidate and spouse as the best fit between the presidential family and institution requires. Marguerite Corbally, wife of the former president of the University of Illinois, suggests why: "It is quite common for the board to direct their discussion of business to the candidate in private and to turn to social subjects when the wife is present. If she has unanswered questions, she may have to be bold in pursuit of the information. The trustees and other constituencies may be unprepared to answer these questions. They may have vague, uncrystallized ideas regarding their expectations of the wife. Some will deny they expect anything of her. Others are hoping that she already knows what is expected without their having to verbalize their uncertain feelings. A few realize that she must be involved, but they want her to feel free to choose. Understandably, most boards are uncomfortable with the subject of the wife because they are not prepared to pay her for her services and they are reluctant to be plain about what they want of her or even to be open about the fact that they do have expectations of her. Some boards give the impression they believe they are hiring only the husband. She may get the impression—and this perception is very commonly reported—that all they wanted with her was to reassure themselves

that she 'looked the part.' "9

This is no longer good enough. If the spouse has no responsibilities with respect to the institution, there is no problem. If he or she has, then both spouse and president should have a clear understanding of what is expected. If there are small children who require the major share of the spouse's time or if he or she wants to pursue an independent career, these factors must be taken into account. They are legitimate limitations on the contribution the spouse can make to the institution.

The terms of the arrangement can of course be negotiated. If the committee or the board is convinced that their situation strongly favors the services of a husband-and-wife team, the candidate must decide whether this is compatible with his and his wife's living style. If the committee or the board is convinced that they have the right person, come what may, they must be prepared to do without the services of the spouse.

There is an additional reason for including the spouse in the interview and in the campus visit. In particular, the spouse will want to look over the community as a place in which to live, the school system, the cultural opportunities, the prospects for continuing his or her own career, the adequacy of the president's house. In short, if the spouse is smart, he or she will want to examine the environment and the expectations as carefully as the committee will want to examine the spouse. The decision to move from one institution or career to another ought to be a joint decision. The wise committee will see that the spouse has his or her many questions answered and will woo the spouse as well as the president.

This section has focused on the president's spouse, but a word needs to be said about the situation where the president has no spouse. This is typical of many Catholic institutions, and it is less uncommon elsewhere than it once was. Committees of selection need to review the demands and pressures on the single president and to make certain that adequate arrangements, satisfactory to the individual and to the institution, can and will be made.

Aftermath of the Visit

At the end of the visit, or immediately thereafter while impressions are fresh, the reactions of people on campus need to be collected. These should be in written form and should be the judgments of individuals, not of groups. The committee of one eastern private college provided faculty and students with forms on which to summarize their reactions under the headings:

- Leadership
- Administrative experience and ability
- Educational philosophy
- Fund raising potential
- Ability to be spokesman for the college
- Dealing with trustees, alumni, faculty, students
- Personal qualities
- Scholarship

The end of the visit is also the time to find out whether the candidate is still actively interested. The candidate may be told that he or she is the committee's first choice or is one of three or four whom the committee is prepared to recommend to the board, and that the committee needs to know whether the candidate will accept the position if offered, or at least the length of time the candidate will need to make a decision.

Some candidates object to this procedure on grounds that the decision is too complex and too momentous to be made unless they are dealing with an actual offer. One can sympathize with this reaction. At the same time it must be recognized that the offer of the presidency is a complex and momentous decision for the trustees. If an offer is made, word usually leaks out. If the offer is turned down, the resulting situation may be awkward if not disastrous. Second and third choices, who under other circumstances would be happy to accept, may withdraw their names. Thus, to protect the reputation of the candidates as well as in their own self-interest, trustees need to know in advance whether the candidate will accept the offer if made.

After the visits, with campus impressions as additional data, the committee must decide on its recommendations. These may be a single name (or more than one), a priority listing, or a slate without ranking—in accordance with the original charge under which the committee has been operating. With this decision the committee completes its major assignment.

There remain for the committee certain chores that are discussed in the last two chapters. Candidates must be notified of the final decision. Announcements must be prepared. A record of the committee's work and an analysis of the number and nature of the candidates considered should be prepared and filed for future reference. Apart from these the final step belongs to the board which must make the appointment and set the terms and conditions.

Additional Sources of Information

Donald E. Fouts: "Picking a President the Business Way," *AGB Reports*, vol. 19, no. 1, January/February 1977.

Marguerite Walker Corbally: *The Partners*, The Interstate Printers and Publishers, Inc. 1977

Joseph F. Kauffman: *The Selection of College and University Presidents*, Association of American Colleges 1974.

_____: "The New College President: Expectations and Realities," *Educational Record*, vol. 58, no. 2, Spring 1977.

Roberta Ostar: "Great Expectations: The President's Spouse," *AGB Reports*, vol. 26, no. 1, January/February 1984.

Joan E. Clodius and Diane Skomars Magrath: *The President's Spouse*, National Association of State Universities and Land-Grant Colleges 1984.

Checklist #7
Selecting Top Candidates

The final selection of the top candidates to be recommended to the board of trustees for serious consideration should be made on the basis of all available evidence, including:

1. A thorough, independent check on the candidates' backgrounds and various job performances. The committee will need to decide:

- **a.** Who should make these inquiries—the chairperson, a committee team, an outside consultant.
- **b.** Whether to proceed by letter, telephone, or on-site visits.
- **c.** How best to safeguard the candidates' privacy (if necessary).
- **d.** Precisely what the committee wants to know.

2. A series of visits to the campus by the candidates unless decision is made to omit them.

- **a.** Why campus visits are important.
- **b.** How many candidates should be invited?
- **c.** The importance of careful scheduling
  - **(1)** For how long?
  - **(2)** Who looks after the candidates?
  - **(3)** Whom should candidates meet?
  - **(4)** What questions should be anticipated from the candidate?
  - **(5)** What documents about institution should be provided candidates?
- **d.** Importance of the visit from the candidate's point of view.
- **e.** Importance of including the candidate's spouse.

3. At the end of the visit, the committee must:

- **a.** Collect and assess the campus reactions.
- **b.** See that the candidate is advised of tentative terms of appointment.
- **c.** Ascertain whether candidate is still actively interested.
- **d.** Make recommendation to board of trustees.

1. Mary Jane McDonald, executive secretary to the college's search committee, in the *Denison Alumnus*, August 1976, vol. 68, no. 1, p. 7.

2. *AGB Reports*, vol. 25, no. 1, January/February 1983, p. 46. Porter's two articles, "Presidential Selection at Large State Universities" in *AGB Reports*, vol. 24, no. 6, November/December 1982, and "The Presidential Search as the Presidents See It" from which the quotation is taken are well worth reading.

3. In our survey we asked the new presidents: "Would you have found a different search and selection process preferable?" Of those who answered either "yes" or "somewhat," 20% gave us the reason inadequate opportunity to get acquainted with the institution and to interact with the various constituencies. One president commented: "My first contact with the search committee was a 40-minute interview in an airport motel suite with the thirteen members of the selection committee. Their next plan was for me to come to the campus for only an afternoon. At my insistence, this was extended to about a 28-hour visit, still not enough."

4. At one campus we visited the committee believed it was important for the host to be present at all the meetings in order to see how consistent the candidate was in the presence of different constituencies.

5. Judith A. Brissette, Board Secretary for Western New England College, in an unpublished doctoral dissertation entitled "A Comparison of the Role of Male and Female Spouses of Presidents of Selected Four-year, Private Colleges," found that a very small percent of spouses were given a chance to discuss their roles with the search committee. She urges committees to address this topic directly with both candidates and spouses.

6. The degree of dissatisfaction reflected by the responses to our survey from the newly elected presidents is disturbing. One can only conclude that a great opportunity is frequently being missed. *See* also Joseph F. Kauffman, "The New College President: Expectations and Realities," in the *Educational Record*, vol. 58, no. 2, Spring 1977, for a thought provoking report on what presidents failed to learn in advance.

7. According to a story in *The Chronicle of Higher Education*, vol. XXIV, no. 8, April 21, 1982, the search for a new chancellor of higher education in Oregon almost fell apart when the number 2 choice withdrew his name after learning through a press leak of his secondary position and the number 1 choice subsequently declined to accept the position allegedly on grounds of inadequate salary and other considerations. Fortunately, the board was able to persuade number 2 to reconsider and accept appointment.

8. It is shocking to discover in the 1983 survey of presidential spouses at public colleges and universities conducted by the American Association of State Colleges and Universities that "46 percent of AASCU campuses with their own boards, and 48 percent of those with system boards, do *not* include the spouse in the interview process." The report is entitled *Myths and Realities* (available from the AASCU office at One Dupont Circle, Washington, D.C. 20036). The quotation is taken from a summary of the findings by Roberta H. Ostar in the January/February 1984 issue of *AGB Reports*, vol. 26, no. 1, title, "Great Expectations: The President's Spouse."

9. *The Partners*, published by Interstate Printers and Publishers, 1977, p. 49, is perhaps the best available analysis of the role of the president's spouse. It ought to be read by every trustee.

Chapter 8

Step Eight— Appointing the President

T he final decision is now in the lap of the board of trustees.

If the selection committee has recommended only one candidate, the board must either ratify or reject the committee's decision. Fortunately, rejection rarely happens. When it does, the committee is asked to try again or is replaced with another committee—with understandable feelings of resentment on the part of the original members.[1] If the committee recommends more than one candidate, the board must make its choice either on the basis of the committee's data and rating or after conducting their own interviews with the candidates. They may, of course, elect to interview some or all of the committee's final candidates even when the committee recommends only one.

Single vs. Multiple Nominations

Should committees of search and selection end up with a single recommendation or should they present to the board of trustees a slate of acceptable candidates? And if the latter, should they rank them in order of preference or, as the trustees of one private university of national stature required, present them in alphabetical order?

For any particular committee the answer lies in the initial charge from the trustees, and this is just one of the many reasons why that charge needs to be stated in unequivocal terms. It is worth noting, however, that quite a few committee chairpersons in our survey reported that, in spite of a mandate to recommend more than one candidate, they had ended up with only one nomination and were able to persuade the trustees to accept their decision. Conversely, one committee with instructions to present a single name was unable to decide between two candidates and passed the buck to the board by nominating them both. The board then made its choice by a four to one decision.

The following table gives the results of our survey of the number of candidates recommended by committees to their respective boards:

	single	where more than one	
4-year public	24%	1-6	3
2-year public	0	3-10	5
private university	50	1-5	3
4-year private	85	1-3	3
4-year church-related	58	1-8	2
2-year private	50	1-3	—

Private college and university boards clearly rely more heavily than public boards on the recommendations of the search and selection committees. The pattern of board decision in public four-year and two-year institutions is further underscored by the fact that in all but one of the four-year public colleges and universities where the selection committee made a single nomination the committee was composed entirely of regents or trustees.

The arguments for a single nomination are obviously quite strong — and in private sector quite persuasive. A conscientious committee will by the end of its labors know more about the candidates and their "fit" with the institution than trustees who have not been directly involved. This position was strongly argued by the chairperson of the committee of a well known church-related college: "When the committee is constituted as ours was to represent trustees (including alumni trustee), faculty, and students—I personally feel that it would be an avoidance of responsibility to recommend several candidates simultaneously. There is no possible way by which other trustees, alumni, faculty, and students could make the same type of careful and prayerful appraisal of the crop of candidates or even three or four of them, as was done by the committee. Any thoughtful committee would be unlikely to find several of equal merit."

Furthermore, a single nomination flatters the nominee. He or she can better endure the leaks in confidentiality that are likely to occur at this final stage since the chances of appointment are high. The risks of turning the selection into a popularity contest, discussed in the previous chapter, are reduced. If the candidate is at all reluctant or undecided, the awareness that he or she is the committee's one choice may be the decisive turning point.

Finally, there is the virtue based on necessity; the committee may have no real choice. The record suggests that committees seeking a slate of candidates not infrequently end up with only one on whom the members can all agree and whom they are prepared to recommend.

On the other hand, a single nomination, in spite of the legal authority of the board to decline to appoint, puts the all important decision in the hands of the search and selection committee. If the trustees or regents are genuinely to exercise the power of appointment, they should have a choice. This is clearly desirable where the committee is composed of nontrustees or where the trustee members play a very minor role. It becomes less important where the committee is dominated by its trustee members, where it has the full confidence of the board, and where the latter has been kept fully informed of the committee's progress.

It is sometimes alleged that the mark of a good committee is its success in finding three or more candidates, all of whom would make in the eyes of the committee satisfactory presidents. Such an outcome is certainly safer, since candidates have a way of withdrawing at the last moment and occasionally the first choice will find the terms of the offer unsatisfactory or will accept an offer from another institution. In such situations, it saves time and possibly embarrassment if the board can turn at once to a second or third choice rather than ask the committee to go into a huddle once again.

The choice between a single recommendation and several will vary from institution to institution. It will depend for some on legislative or bylaw regulations. For others the temper of the institution will determine the choice. A high degree of mutual trust among the various constituencies, general agreement on the kind of person wanted and needed, the absence of divisive forces politicizing the campus tend toward placing major responsibility in the committee of selection. Where these conditions do not obtain, it is better for the trustees to have a choice of candidates and to be recognized as making the decision.

It is presumably this emphasis on the role of the trustees that leads some boards to request an unranked slate of names, but it is difficult to see either need or justification for it. If a committee cannot agree on its order of preference, which means that the members of the committee disagree on the merits of the candidates, it may simply present a list of possible names. In most cases, however, members of the committee will be able to agree on their ranking of candidates, and the board should have the benefit of their judgment. It may be, for example, that candidates A and B are virtually equal in the committee's eyes and C some distance below them; or A may be way out in front with the rest bunched well behind. This is information the trustees should have.

The Board Appointment

Presidents are appointed by boards, and therefore, the final act in the search and selection scenario is the official board decision. It is a decision that should be made by the full board. The board is free to reject the recommendations of its committee, but doing so is likely to raise a hornet's nest of difficulties. Members of the committee, who presumably have worked long and hard trying to find the right person, are going to be unhappy. If the board makes no appointment, committee members may refuse to try again, in which case a new committee must be formed to start all over. If the board appoints someone not recommended by the committee, the incoming president may find himself or herself the target of suspicion and hostility by the constituencies represented on the committee.

The board may wish to conduct its own interviews with one or more finalists, particularly if few trustees have had a prior opportunity of meeting the candidates. Or the board may have such confidence in the search and selection committee(s) that the board is willing to act on the recommendations presented. In making the appointment the board should confirm the terms negotiated or vote authority to the chairperson or some special board committee to settle the terms of employment. The former is clearly to be preferred to the latter.

Terms of Appointment

Terms of appointment is a broad phrase dealing with a wide variety of conditions and circumstances not always considered by either board or president at the time of decision. Indeed, less thought seems to be given to these matters than to the business of selection. Agreement is frequently postponed until circumstances force a decision.

In the majority of situations good will and common sense prevail, but our survey turned up disturbing evidence of expectations on the part of the presidents—and even promises—that were not fulfilled, leading to disappointment and disillusion.[2] A lot of heartache, dissaffection, and future trouble would be avoided if boards, and chancellors in statewide systems, were clearer and more specific at time of appointment on the practical and professional arrangements for the new presidents. These fall into three groups: (1) financial, (2) professional, and (3) administrative.

(1) Financial

The financial offer should cover most (though not necessarily all) of the following items:

    salary
    annuity or pension provisions
    medical or health insurance
    life insurance
    moving expenses
    president's house plus
        maintenance and repairs
        or housing allowance
    household help
    entertainment expenses
    automobile and expenses
    travel expenses
    secretarial help for spouse

Some of these items need little comment. Provision for retirement income, whether through TIAA-CREF or a state employee pension plan or some institutionally funded plan, is standard. Many medical or health insurance programs include some provision for life insurance. It is customary to provide moving expenses for the new president and his or her family.

Since the nature of the president's job requires extensive travel, the costs should be reimbursed. Perceptive boards will encourage wife or husband to travel with the president by covering the spouse's travel costs as well, state law permitting in the case of tax-supported institutions.

Housing for the president and his or her family varies widely. Many institutions—for example, the majority of community colleges and some of the smaller private and church-related colleges—make no provision, it being assumed that the president's salary is sufficient to provide for this as well as other family expenses. Many institutions, however, do provide a president's house as part of the compensation packet and because they expect the president to carry on a certain amount of official entertaining in his or her home. This is often a larger and more expensive establishment than the individual would choose. Since the house belongs to the college or university, it should be understood that repairs and normal maintenance are the responsibility of the institution. This may apply as well to domestic service and to the not inconsiderable costs of official entertaining. At least there should be clear understanding from the start as to who pays for what.

In some cases, the official residence may not be suitable, and other arrangements will need to be made—and agreed upon in advance. In periods of inflation presidents may prefer to own their own houses in order to develop equity against the time when they will have to fend for themselves.

An official automobile is an optional item. It is fairly common for public four-year institutions to make one available. So do many of the larger and better financed private colleges and universities.

Also optional is secretarial help for the president's spouse. At the university level the demand on his or her services—for entertaining, for community functions, for meetings of one sort or another—may be so great that a private secretary, full-time or part-time, may be essential. Where this is not considered necessary or appropriate, the availability of secretarial help from one of the college offices should be agreed to as part of the working conditions.[3]

(2) Professional

Academic administration is a professional job. With the exception of a few individuals drawn from business, the military, law, or the ministry, college and university presidents are pursuing a professional career in education—a career that usually begins with teaching and progresses through various educational and administrative steps to the presidency. Continued professional growth is extremely important not only to the president's effectiveness in his or her present assignment, but also in anticipation of a postpresidential career. Boards of trustees need to make provision for this need in terms of:

> adequate vacation
> leaves of absence
> extramural activities
> professional competence

Provision for a formal vacation period should be part of the contract or letter of appointment. One month is normal, but sometimes six weeks or two months are agreed upon, especially where the president uses some of the "vacation" time for writing annual reports or making studies that cannot be efficiently pursued in the midst of campus pressures. Chairpersons need to keep a friendly eye on the emotional and nervous condition of their presidents and should encourage them to take occasional breaks from the time-consuming demands of their office. Business executives restore their energy and drive and gain perspective on broad issues by taking winter as well as summer holidays: college and university presidents need periodic opportunities for recuperation, too. In the long run the institution gains thereby.

In 1971 the Association of American Colleges adopted a statement on administrative leaves of absence which reads in part: "Because of the unique position of the president and the special planning required for implementation of a presidential leave, the governing board of the institution should assume responsibility for initiating this leave program and provide special funding to support it." The resolution emphasizes that the president should not be required to apply for a leave as though it were a special favor. It concludes: "As for any administrative leave, the precise terms of a presidential leave should be agreed to and stated in writing in advance."

Presidential leaves are less uncommon today than was formerly the case. Their value is being more widely recognized. Trustees are becoming more concerned to get the maximum return on their human investment. "Given the substantial investment a governing board makes in finding a president," writes Joseph Kauffman, "it is simp-

ly good management for the board to conserve this important resource. Leadership is a scarce and precious asset that should not be taken for granted."[4]

Just as some college and university presidents continue to teach — a practice that, however desirable and laudable, is becoming increasingly difficult to manage— so others will continue active participation in professional societies and conferences. In due course, others will be invited to serve on corporate and foundation boards. Federal, state, and local agencies may request service on special public service commissions or panels. All these serve to keep professional interests alive and enlarging. They add new dimensions to the presidents' stature, new perspectives to their understanding of contemporary society. Active participation in religious organizations is not only an extramural outlet for the individual, but may also be an important contribution to the institution—especially for the president of a church-related college. Presidents, who have little leisure for reflection, should seize opportunities for the kind of extracurricular activities that will give them perspective on their jobs. The need for this cannot be written into a contract, but its value should be recognized by the board.

Staying alive professionally is also an important hedge against the day when the president may want other employment. With an average tenure between 6 and 6½ years most presidents are unlikely to continue to the point of retirement unless they are in the last decade of their normal life. The Commission on Strengthening Presidential Leadership referred to in a footnote in the Introduction contends that current tenures in office are too short for the exercise of real educational leadership and recommends various changes calculated to lengthen presidential tenure. The president may, of course, move on to another college or university presidency, but it may well be a return to former professional work or to a related field. The more professionally competent, the greater the likelihood of a successful transition.

(3) Administrative

Lumped under this general heading are the following:
- starting date
- retirement date
- length of appointment
- conditions of termination
- criteria of performance
- provision for review and evaluation

The starting date normally presents no difficulty, though it may need to be negotiated if the college or university is facing a sudden crisis or if the president-elect has commitments that cannot be gracefully cancelled.

Unless the institution's bylaws or a board resolution specify the age of retirement for administrative officers as well as faculty, the appropriate date of retirement for the incoming president (on the assumption, of course, that all will go well) should be discussed, and the proper time for settling this matter is prior to or at the time of appointment.

It should be clearly understood that all presidential appointments are at the pleasure of the board, for once the trustees have lost confidence in the president, the good of the institution requires his or her departure. There was a time when presidents were appointed for life, or at least for a pleasantly indefinite future. The figure on average tenure previously cited suggests that boards today would be wise to proceed on different assumptions.

Should presidential appointments be formally renewed year by year? Should they be for an indefinite period? Should they run for a given term of, say, five years?

In recent years, there has been a distinct trend toward term appointments. Clark Kerr, former president of the University of California and former chairman of the Carnegie Council on Policy Studies on Higher Education, recommends that the president be given "a term appointment of reasonable length. This will give him, except under exceptional circumstances, a fixed period on which he can plan. At the end of the term, he will have an easy opportunity to review his own desires and for others to review his conduct. If he is reappointed, he will have received a reaffirmation of his authority as he meets new crises. In any event, opponents will not feel that they must wait forever for a change unless they mount massive opposition. A term of office could relax their opposition."[5]

Warren Bennis takes a similar line, arguing that term appointments give presidents more freedom and authority to take risks in new educational ventures, to stand up to opposition—in short to exercise the kind of leadership so widely demanded in theory and so extensively opposed in practice. He further points out that skills and styles go quickly out of fashion in contemporary society, so that both the institution and the individual need to reappraise the situation every so often.[6]

Whether a board appoints the president for a given term, which may of course be renewed, or for an indefinite period, it must realistically assume that the president is not likely to remain forever. It would be nice to have the president continue for ten to fifteen years, but ten or fewer years is the likely prospect. Whether the departure occurs in accordance with some agreed upon schedule or as the result of board dissatisfaction with the president's performance, plans for the separation need to be laid in advance.

Boards and candidates assume, as do people getting married, that their lives together will be harmonious. They look to the future with confidence. It seems, therefore, slightly indecent to want to discuss what they should do if they find that they cannot live and work together. Yet, this is precisely what is needed. The board needs to know that the new president will not desert the ship at short notice, and the president needs assurance that he or she will be given reasonable leave with salary if the axe should fall. Further, the absence of clear terminal arrangements can lead to lawsuits, which are expensive and produce bad publicity.

The sensible board will anticipate the possibility of trouble, however remote it may seem, and set forth the terms, conditions and circumstances of separation at the time of appointment. "Provision should be made at the beginning of a president's term for the possibility of termination," writes Charles C. Cole, Jr. "Ample severance pay, a period for the smooth transition of responsibilities, assistance in relocation, the phasing out of such fringe benefits as hospitalization and disability insurance—these are stipulations that it would be well to work out amiably rather than in a time of crisis when feelings may be strained and perspectives warped."[7]

What form should the agreement between the board and the new president take? With the exception of only one group, the most widely used form is a letter from the board chairperson (or the chief executive officer in a statewide system) to the candidate setting forth the terms and conditions. The one exception consists of community colleges where formal contracts are the rule.

What is really surprising is the number of institutions where the agreement is entirely oral. One would expect to find this occasionally in private institutions. The president of one such institution where arrangements had been exclusively oral commented: "The information was sufficient in terms of my requirements. Others might prefer a more formal understanding." But in 11% of the four-year public institutions and 12% of the two-year no written agreements were exchanged.

Some formal written statement covering the terms of the appointment ought to be made in every instance. "I would give no one a contract," wrote one board chairman who nevertheless set forth the terms in a letter to the president. The difference between a contract and a contractual letter is a fine one, but the difference between a written and oral agreement is the difference between a good operation and a sloppy one.

There is no standard contract or contractual letter covering the many items just discussed, but with a checklist of points to be covered it should not be difficult to draw up a satisfactory statement of agreement. Most of the chairpersons in our survey reported that they had made clear the terms of appointment, but it was obvious from the responses of the presidents that a third of them felt the reverse. To a large extent this negative reaction was based on a failure by the board to set forth the criteria by which presidents' performances would be judged, and we shall now deal with that topic in a separate section.

Criteria of Selection and Performance Review

Surprising, indeed shocking, as sometimes appears the laxity regarding practical terms of employment, the almost complete absence of statements on criteria of performance is astounding. The litany of presidential comments is disturbing.

"Matters of compensation were clearly set forth at the time of my appointment. 'Criteria of performance' were not, nor was a term of service specified. The mores of this board do not allow for negotiations of this kind."

"Salary and fringe benefits by letter of intent. No criteria of performance have been agreed upon—or stated. There is little uniformity in expectations and in criteria of performance."

"The board agreed to review of performance in the fifth year, but they never clearly spelled out the criteria to be used or the method."

"No information provided on criteria of performance. These clearly have been shif-

ting and vary within the membership of the board as well as with faculty, students, and alumnae."

An occasional chairperson in our survey recognized that the board had not addressed itself to what the president was expected to do. The disturbing feature is that so many seemed unaware of any problem. "To run the college," one can hear them saying. "To direct the affairs of the university." Those are noble goals but inadequate yardsticks by which to judge whether the president is doing his or her job.

To repeat what is obvious, and too frequently ignored: the president is the agent of the board of trustees or regents. The board sets the policies—very often at the president's instigation and always, one hopes, with the president's participation. Within the policies so laid down, the president must operate and it is the board's responsibility to judge whether the president operates well or ill. How can the president know what is expected and how can the trustees judge how well the president has lived up to expectations unless there is prior agreement on what the institution needs?

"Standards of performance are the basis for review," writes James L. Hayes, chairperson of the board of St. Bonaventure University and president of the American Management Associations. "In effect, we always review performance rather than the individual. When we do not have standards, then personal characteristics and emotional chemistry as well as politics take over and the system fails or justice falters.

"Standards should be negotiated with the incumbent if they were not a basis for hiring, and usually they are not. We still tend to hire to position descriptions which allow for wide interpretations of standards."

In recent years there has been a trend toward formal assessment of presidential performance—an open, public, periodic review. The results have not been particularly encouraging. Whether formal or informal, judgments of presidential performance are constantly being made. The president has a right to know by what criteria he or she will be judged. The trustees have an obligation to make them clear. If they have done the job of analyzing the future needs and problems of the institution, discussed in Chapters 1 and 3 as the only proper basis for selecting a new president, board members should be able to convert the results into a set of expectations for presidential performance on which a fair and intelligent appraisal can be based.

Announcing the Appointment

The choice has been made, the terms agreed upon, and the appointment made official. There remains the public announcement, which is an institutional responsibility, and the private notification to unsuccessful candidates, which belongs to the committee. The two aspects need to be coordinated.

Excitement will be high and rumors rampant. There is every reason for making a public announcement at the earliest possible date. That date must allow the president-elect time to notify his or her colleagues and superiors before they read about the appointment in the newspapers.

It must also allow time for the selection committee to notify any finalists who have not already been bowed out of the picture. If only a few remain, telephone calls will be the most gracious way of informing them of the choice. No one who has any reason to believe he or she might still be in the running should learn of the decision by newspaper or radio.

Faculty, students, administrative staff should be informed before the public announcement.

News releases will need to be prepared and distributed at the proper time. Copies might be sent to all candidates and to those who have nominated candidates—with appropriate cover letters thanking them for their interest and help. A little extra effort at this point will enhance the reputation and standing of the institution.

Alumni will need to be informed either by special announcement from the committee or the chairperson of the board, or by an article (in the alumni magazine) reviewing the search, selection, and appointment.

Two examples of typical announcements are appended as Exhibits S and T.

Additional Sources of Information

Warren Bennis: *The Leaning Ivory Tower*, Jossey-Bass Publishers 1973, Chapter 4.

Michael D. Cohen and James G. March: *Leadership and Ambiguity—The American College President*, McGraw-Hill 1974, Chapter 8.

Charles C. Cole, Jr.: "The Reeling Presidency" in *Educational Record*, vol. 57, no. 2, Spring 1976.

David L. McKenna: "Recycling College Presidents" in *Liberal Education*, vol. 58, no. 4, December 1972.

————— : "Ten Lessons of a Recycled President" in *Liberal Education*, vol. 63, no. 3, October 1977.

Joseph F. Kauffman: *The Selection of College and University Presidents*, Association of American Colleges 1974.

Clark Kerr: "Presidential Discontent" in *Perspectives on Campus Tensions*, American Council on Education 1970.

"Guidelines for Conditions of Employment for College and University Presidents"—Policy Statement adopted by the American Association of State Colleges and Universities 1957.

Preliminary 1983/1984 Compensation and Benefits Survey of College and University Chief Executive Officers, April 1984, prepared for the Association of Governing Boards of Universities and Colleges and College and University Personnel Association, by Sibson & Company, Inc. of Princeton, New Jersey.

Checklist #8
Appointing the President

1. The appointment is made by the board of trustees. Should the board act on a single recommendation from the selection committee or make its choice from among a slate of candidates? Single choice is more common in private institutions. Multiple choice is more the rule in public ones.

  a. Advantages of single choice
- **(1)** Committee knows candidates better than board.
- **(2)** Encourages candidate to accept.
- **(3)** Works well where board trusts committee.

  b. Arguments for multiple choice:
- **(1)** Places responsibility for choice squarely on board.
- **(2)** Avoids embarassing delay if first choice withdraws or declines.

  c. If committee recommends slate of candidates, board should have benefit of committee's ranking.

2. When, by whom, and how should terms of appointment be set?

  a. By discussion with committee before recommendation?

  b. By board chairperson before board decision is reached?

  c. At time offer is made?

  d. Avoid awkwardness of leaving negotiations on terms until after offer has been made and accepted.

  e. How should agreement be stated?
- **(1)** Orally, i.e. gentlemen's agreement.
- **(2)** By letter from chairperson or chancellor in state system.
- **(3)** By formal contract.

3. The terms of the appointment should cover all or most of the following items:

a. Financial
- **(1)** salary
- **(2)** annuity or pension provisions, medical or health insurance
- **(3)** life insurance
- **(4)** moving expenses
- **(5)** president's house plus maintenance and repairs
- **(6)** household help
- **(7)** entertainment expense
- **(8)** automobile and expenses
- **(9)** travel expenses
- **(10)** secretarial help for spouse

b. Professional
- **(1)** vacation
- **(2)** leaves of absence
- **(3)** extramural activities
- **(4)** professional competence

c. Administrative
- **(1)** starting date
- **(2)** retirement date
- **(3)** length of appointment
- **(4)** conditions of termination
- **(5)** criteria of performance
- **(6)** provision for review and evaluation

4. The public announcement:

a. Timing—as early as possible

b. Inform top candidates *before* public announcement

c. Decide who and how information will be distributed to
- **(1)** general public
- **(2)** campus community
- **(3)** roster of candidates and those who proposed candidates
- **(4)** alumni

---

1. At one private university, the search was conducted by an advisory committee consisting of faculty, students, alumni, and administrators, but not trustees. The committee concluded that it could recommend only one candidate. At the insistence of the board, the committee reluctantly presented three names, reiterating that they thought only one was acceptable. The board then interviewed all three and chose one who was not recommended. The advisory committee ended up with fifteen bitter people, according to its chairperson.

2. Consider the comment of the president of an institution in a statewide system in response to the question whether the terms of appointment had been made clear: "Vague letter of appointment from governor. Unfulfilled expectations were a source of frustration and disappointment. Benefits promised—maid service, car and meals—not forthcoming because of misunderstanding at board of state system." Housing is a frequent source of misunderstanding and unhappiness.

3. See the Preliminary 1983/84 Compensation and Benefits Survey of College and University Chief Executive Officers, prepared for the Association of Governing Boards of Universities and Colleges and College and University Personnel Association, April 1984, for information on current practices.

4. *The Selection of College and University Presidents*, p. 61. *See* also two articles by David L. McKenna: "Recycling College Presidents" in *Liberal Education*, vol. 58, no. 4, December 1972; and "Ten Lessons of a Recycled President," vol. 63, no. 3, October 1977. Charles C. Cole, Jr., former president of Wilson College, analyzes the reasons for the resignations of 118 college and university presidents in the academic year 1975-76 in an article entitled "The Reeling Presidency," *Educational Record*, vol. 57, no. 2, Spring 1976. One of his conclusions is that presidents must learn to pace themselves in order to avoid exhaustion. "It is essential that busy presidents take leaves of absence and brief holidays for mental and emotional rest and refreshment. It is crucial not be thrown off balance."

5. "Presidential Discontent" in *Perspectives on Campus Tensions*, American Council on Education 1970, pp. 159-60.

6. *The Leaning Ivory Tower*, Jossey-Bass Publishers 1973, pp. 82-83.

7. "The Reeling Presidency," *Educational Record*, vol. 57, no. 2, Spring 1976, p. 76.

Chapter 9

Step Nine—
Winding Down
and Gearing Up

Before the excitement has quite subsided and the dust completely settled, there are a few final steps to be taken.

Preserving the Record

For the guidance of future committees a final and relatively complete report of the whole process should be drafted and filed. Sometimes the chairperson of the committee assumes this responsibility; more often it is done by the committee's secretary or an administrative staff member.

The search and selection of the new president is a very important event in the life of a college or university. Some future historian of the institution will welcome the light that a summary report will shed on a long-past event. But, it will also serve a purpose in the nearer future. Memories quickly grow dim and erratic. Papers get lost or mislaid. Indeed, the confidential documents regarding candidates should either be destroyed or filed under lock and key for some set period of years. The committee obviously hopes that another search will not have to be undertaken for a long time to come. The chances are that, when it does occur, the committee will consist of entirely different people. A detailed report on procedures, problems, and conclusions—which might well contain a section on what not to do—will be invaluable to the new committee.

An example of the sort of information that might be included in such a report is the following list of documents attached to a three-page summary of the composition mode of operation, and conclusions of an unusually well-organized committee:

1. Excerpt from *Trustees in Higher Education* by Gerald P. Burns, Independent College Funds 1966.

2. Flow Chart (indicating process of finding and selecting candidates).

3. Charge to Committee

4. Membership of Committee

5. Criteria of Selection

6. Recruiting Plan

7. Job Description

8. Advertisement and Information About

9. Letter Seeking Nominations

10. Letter from Chairman of the Board to Alumni and Parents

11. Memo on Legal Requirements

12. Mailing Lists

13. Outline Method for Handling Papers

14. Forms Used for Processing Information

15. Forms Used for Scheduling

16. List of Questions for Telephone Interviews (for candidates reaching final stage)

17. Report to Equal Employment Opportunity Commission

18. Letter to Applicants (Thanks for)

19. Letter to Nominators (Thanks for)

20. Summary Report

For institutions holding federal contracts Executive Order 11246 requires that data pertaining to equal opportunity be preserved. In a memorandum explaining federal requirements the Director of the Office of Civil Rights in 1975 wrote: "The Executive Order establishes the principle that federal contrac-

tors, including collegs and universities, are required to collect and maintain data on the race, sex, and ethnic identity of all applicants for employment. The collection and analysis of such data is recognized as an essential means of providing both the institution and the federal government with the information necessary to monitor the compliance posture of the institution."[1]

Easing the Transition

The committee's work is now done, but someone—trustees or staff or faculty or some combination thereof—should be prepared to help the new president make a good start.

Unless the president-elect is an insider, there will be problems of transition from the old regime to the new. The new president will have much to learn about his or her new responsibilities. Since the outgoing president will normally try to leave maximum flexibility for his or her successor by making as few long-term decisions as possible, the incoming president will be faced with more than the normal run of important decisions.

Where the transition is a friendly one, the outgoing president can be expected to counsel with his or her successor on critical issues, booby traps, and the like. Exhibit U is a memorandum from a private college officer suggesting to the departing president various steps that would be of help to the new president and an advantage to the college.

A transition team or committee, as suggested in the memorandum, might be appointed to serve for the first six months of the new president's regime. This might include the faculty members on the search and selection committee. If a committee is not advisable, a senior and respected member of the faculty might be asked to serve as special counselor to the president, to be called on for advice and inside information whenever needed. It is extremely important that the new president start off in the right direction, for the first decisions and the first speeches to faculty, staff, and students will be examined very carefully and to a large extent will determine campus opinion.

One of the most difficult problems for new presidents, according to the findings of the Commission on Strengthening Presidential Leadership, is the number of untouchables on the administrative staff. The new president, if wise, will try hard to work with the administrative team he or she inherits, but long established administrative officers do not always cotton to new ideas and sometimes are reluctant to change their ways. The new president is entitled to form his or her own administrative staff in due course and should be free to make changes designed to improve administrative effectiveness. Change becomes not only difficult but for all practical purposes impossible unless the chairperson of the board is prepared to support the president.

Some new presidents face disappointed candidates within the institution. At best this can be an awkward situation; at worst it is disastrous. The politics of academia can be as brutal as anywhere else. The new president can expect a certain amount of aloofness bordering on hostility, but any attempts at obstruction or campaigns of denigration should be scotched at once—

and not by the new president. It is the responsibility of the trustees, and especially of the chairperson, to monitor the situation, to counsel closely with the president, and to take steps, sometimes drastic steps, to prevent sabotage of programs and to stop the rise of factionalism.

If the president-elect has not had extensive administrative experience, he or she may be lacking in certain technical tools of the trade. Sometimes the president-elect will take the initiative in proposing one or more management training courses, but often the chairperson will need to encourage the new president to attend special institutes or conferences in areas where the president needs support.

In Conclusion

The analysis and recommendations contained in this study of presidential selection have emphasized time and again the importance of the selection process in the life of the institution. For everyone concerned, the choice of a new president has traumatic implications.

The analysis of institutional needs on which the criteria for the new president are based can unite trustees, faculty, administration, students, alumni and state educational officers on the mission of the college or university. The long and intense work of trustees, faculty, students and others on the search and selection committees breeds mutual understanding, and understanding breeds trust. Many chairpersons in our survey testified to the healing and harmonizing effects of close cooperation in a common cause. And we hope that we have made the point that the manner in which the committee communicates with candidates, with those suggesting candidates, and with references for candidates says something important about the nature and style of the institution. What can seem to be by-products of the selection process turn out to be among its most valuable (or damaging) results.

Our purpose in examining the various ways in which college and university presidents have been selected has been to extract certain guidelines for the most effective procedures. These will vary in detail from one type of institution to another, but the broad principles of what constitutes good practice remain the same for all. We hope that the analysis and recommendations here set forth will facilitate and improve the process, thereby strengthening colleges and universities at a critical point in their lives.

---

1. See NACUBO *Guide to Federal Regulations* (June 30, 1978) prepared by Hanson and Pondrum, described in Chapter 4, footnote 3, of this study.

EXHIBIT A

Sample Four-Month Timetable

January 11	The executive committee authorizes the chairperson of the board of trustees to name a presidential selection committee.
January 23	The selection committee is appointed and approved by the executive committee and includes five trustees, two faculty members, an associate, and a student.
January 24	The board of trustees confirms the action of the executive committee.
January 24	The selection committee meets for the first time to develop and approve two statements: one describing the institution, the other detailing the attributes sought in a candidate.
February	Nominations and applications are solicited through journals and other news publications, the various institution constituencies, other college and university administrators, and foundations and educational associations.
February and March	The selection committee meets to review and assess the files of active candidates. Initial interviews are conducted.
February, March and April	Campus interviews for serious candidates are scheduled with the selection committee and the various advisory groups.
April 25	The selection committee meets for final selection of a candidate.
May 15	The selection committee recommends a candidate to the executive committee.

EXHIBIT B

Sample Eight-Month Timetable

Mid-September	Announcement of president's resignation as of following June.
September 15 to October 15	Appointment and organization of search and selection committee—strategy, criteria, preparation of ads, and list of individuals to get requests for nominations.
October 15-30	Advertisements in *Chronicle*, local newspapers, and special journals.
November and December	Screening of applicants and nominees as they come in. Three lists of possible candidates with priority list of 20.
Late December-early January	Committee travel to east and west coasts to talk with nominated candidates and to get further nominations from special friends of institution.
January	Committee meetings for stock taking—review of new names from trip, further background information.
February and March	Screened priority list to 7. Pursued background information, off-campus interviews.
March-early April	Interviewed 7 candidates on campus—6 privately and finally one exposed to college community.
End of April	Recommended one candidate to board.
Mid-May	Board met and made appointment.

EXHIBIT C
Sample Search Budget

Committee Staff Salaries	
Executive Secretary—part time	$ 6,000
Clerk/Typist—part time	4,000
Office Expenses	
Stationery and supplies	750
Telephone	1,000
Postage	500
Typewriter rental	450
Consultant Fees and Expenses	16,500
Advertising	
The Chronicle of Higher Education	900
Candidate Travel	
10 off-campus interviews	4,000
3 candidate/spouse visits to campus	2,500
Committee Travel	
Off-campus interviews	1,500
Site visit(s) to finalists	1,000
Committee meetings—travel & lodging	1,200
Contingency	1,200
Total	$41,500

EXHIBIT D

Institutional Profile

The following is the profile of institutional concerns and problems on which the search committee of a midwestern liberal arts college based its criteria for its new president:

I. Reputation and Identity

1. To remain academically strong, innovative, flexible and devoted to the liberal arts.
2. To develop and publicize a strong case for liberal arts education.
3. To retain the present level of excellence in the faculty.
4. To analyze and evaluate the institution's appeal to its present constituencies.

II. Enrollment and Finances

1. To carry out an intense development campaign with these main goals:
   a. To substantially increase endowment.
   b. To augment scholarship funds.
2. To maintain student enrollment at or near 2,000.
3. To examine and, where necessary, improve our teaching in order to engage the full capacities of the students actually enrolled; the goal is to provide quality liberal arts education to all students, including those whose academic talent or preparation is less than that of students we have been able to attract in the past.

III. Communication and Trust

1. External: To improve communication and trust between members of the university community and trustees, alumni, parents, neighbors and society in general, in order to elicit commitment to our institutional purposes and aspirations and meet some of the expectations of friends of the college.
2. Internal: To improve communication and trust among members of our academic community, specifically, students, faculty, administrators, and supportive/operating staff, in order to understand, participate in and support the programs, decisions, and goals of one another.

IV. Diversity

1. *Of Faculty:* To increase the number of women and minority faculty members.
2. *Of Students:* To increase heterogeneity of student body by attracting students from diverse economic, ethnic, and social backgrounds.
3. *Of Trustees:* To attract trustees of different backgrounds in order to provide a mix that will encourage creative attention to the varied needs and characteristics of the college.

V. Discussion and Decision

1. To decide what our responsibilities are with regard to students' vocational concerns.
2. To better understand what motivates students and to respond creatively to such knowledge.
3. To decide where there is need for integration of knowledge and to create new interdisciplinary opportunities for students where this is appropriate.
4. To examine ways in which our isolation affects student life.

VI. Physical Plant

1. *No* need for new physical plant; need to maintain the campus at its present level of cleanliness, repair, and beauty.
2. Need to improve efficiency of use of physical plant; to explore extramural uses for campus facilities.
3. Need to conserve energy and reduce the university's impact on the environment.
4. Need to improve facilities in the arts, to provide more opportunities for students to make creative use of leisure time.

EXHIBIT E
Presidential Profile

The following criteria used by the selection committee of an eastern women's college gives evidence that they were based on an institutional assessment:

The selection committee is particularly interested in finding a person who has the desire to continue the current directions and momentum of the college and the leadership potential to chart new courses as opportunities develop. More specifically, the college seeks an individual with all or most of the following attributes.

Someone who:

• is dedicated to the growth and strengthening of contemporary women's education,

• believes that the solid core of liberal arts can be amplified through the development and expansion of career and professional programs,

• understands the benefits of college involvement in community and regional problems and the value of internships in providing students with a wide and rich range of off-campus work/study opportunities,

• is committed to modern management, endorsing a delegated division of labor, a management team approach, and a wide dissemination of information,

• places value on up-to-date planning, programming and budgetary processes as an important and effective tool for managing college finances,

• is capable of effectively developing financial support from outside sources,

• accepts the principle of student self-governance in student affairs,

• is able to work effectively with the diverse constituencies of the college,

• has proven administrative and academic experience, and

• has earned the highest academic degree.

EXHIBIT F

FROM: Vice President and General Counsel
TO: Chairman, Search Committee
CC: Affirmative Action Coordinator
Search Committee Coordinator
Secretary of Search Committee
President
Provost, Affirmative Action Officer

RE: LEGAL REQUIREMENTS GUIDE FOR PRESIDENTIAL SEARCH COMMITTEE

I note below the legal requirements with respect to equal employment and affirmative action which should guide the search committee in its work. . . .

1. The job description may not in any way limit applications on the basis of race, religion, national origin or sex.

2. Any advertisement of the vacancy must note that Bucknell is an equal opportunity and affirmative action employer.

3. A good faith effort must be made to seek applicants of both sexes and to provide an opportunity for application from minority groups. This requirement is usually satisfied by advertising in publications of general circulation such as the educational section of *The New York Times, The Chronicle of Higher Education,* etc. It would be appropriate, however, to advertise as well in publications which might bring the vacancy to the attention of women applicants, or to notify women's organizations or minority organizations of the existence of the vacancy. I suggest that copies of our *New York Times* advertisements and of the job description should be sent to each such agency. A record should be maintained of all publication of the notice and of a list to whom such information has been sent.

4. No inquiry should be made about marital status.

5. A record should be maintained on the race, sex, and ethnic identity of applicants. It will be necessary to include such information in a report on the search. This implies that a full record should be maintained of the number of

applicants by category. The committee should likewise be prepared to report on the disposition of applications and to justify the selection of a white male on the basis of his qualifications over any female or minority applicants and their qualifications if such should so be the final decision.

6. In the above comments, no reference is made to age. Nonetheless, within the limit set by university retirement policies, there may be no discrimination based on age in the stated job description or criteria for employment.

7. A written job description should be prepared which includes anticipated responsibilities and qualifications. Special attention should be given to insure that qualifications based on education, experience or other skills do not in themselves constitute discrimination.

8. Before candidates are interviewed, the institution's committee on equal employment opportunity must approve the job description, and before an offer of employment is made to a person who does not fill one of the goals of the plan, the committee must review the offer to certify that the requirements of the university's affirmative action plan have been met. The committee should furnish the Coordinator with a copy of its recruiting plan—i.e., a list of the media in which advertisements have been placed, offices to which notices have been sent, etc. before a list of candidates for interviews is compiled. The coordinator of the affirmative action plan maintains standard forms for reports on recruiting and is required to report annually on all recruiting activities. The committee should furnish the coordinator with the results of its work.

Good luck!

EXHIBIT G

Mr. John Smith
President
Hampshire College
Amherst, Massachusetts 01002

Dear Mr. Smith:

President Longsworth's departure from Hampshire College on June 30, 1977 to become the President of the Colonial Williamsburg Foundation presents everyone at Hampshire College with a large challenge and an exciting opportunity. The challenge is to select a person who can meet the measure of innovation and creativity set by Chuck and his predecessor Franklin Patterson. The opportunity is to find a person who can build on their work and lead Hampshire to realize its great promise.

We know that our job will be difficult.

We solicit your assistance.

Specifically, we would greatly appreciate it if you would send us the names of people you consider qualified to be Hampshire's president. Please direct your corresondence to me at:

    Box A
    Hampshire College
    Amherst, Massachusetts 01002

Enclosed, for your information, is a statement describing the nature of the position and the kind of person who might fill it well.

I am clear that we ask no little favor; we shall be grateful for your consideration of our important need.

Sincerely,

John P. Kendall
Chairman of the Board of Trustees

JPK/pjm
Encl.

EXHIBIT H

Dear President _____ :

The Board of Regents of Eastern Kentucky University is seeking a successor to President Robert R. Martin who will retire effective October 1, 1976. Dr. Martin has served as the sixth president of the University since 1960.

We are requesting you, as one of a selected list of chief administrators in higher education, to assist us in filling this position. We will be deeply grateful for your nomination of one or more candidates, either from your own campus or from some other location. You may assure the nominee that names and vitae will be handled in professional confidence. It would be helpful to have any supporting statement you wish to make, but if you prefer to furnish only name and address, we will extend an invitation for submission of application and resume. We expect to have all applications in hand no later than July 1, 1976, and nominations or applications may be mailed to:

> Presidential Search Committee
> Post Office Box 2000
> Richmond, Kentucky 40475

The enclosed materials provide information regarding the position, the University, and the geographic area in which Eastern Kentucky University is located.

Your assistance and nomination of qualified persons will be genuinely appreciated by the Presidential Search Committee.

Sincerely,

Robert B. Begley
Co-Chairman

RBB/jwh

Enclosure

EXHIBIT I
Model Letter A:

To all sponsors of all nominees who can be contacted directly. Letter will be sent personal and confidential.

Date

Dear _____ :

Thank you very much for your nomination of _____ as candidate for president of X College. We appreciate your effort on our behalf and your interest in the College.

The search committee is now evaluating candidates and expects to reach a decision after the first of the year. We will notify you of the final decision.

Thank you again for your interest and help.

Sincerely yours,

Chairman
Presidential Search Committee

EXHIBIT J
Model Letter B:

To sponsor of any candidate who can't be contacted directly. Letter will be sent personal and confidential.

Date

Dear _____

Thank you for proposing _____ as a candidate for the presidency of X College. In order to respect _____'s current position, we have not contacted (him/her) directly. It would, therefore, be helpful to us if you could determine whether or not _____ is interested in being considered as a candidate. If so, we ask you to provide a supporting statement which includes the following:

- An up-to-date *curriculum vita* of the candidate, if not already provided.
- Your reasons for proposing the nominee for this particular position.
- The names and addresses from whom useful information about the nominee can be secured and whose endorsement you feel might strengthen your proposal.
- The capacity in which you have known the candidate.

We enclose a Statement of Criteria for the President of X College which may be helpful to you in formulating your response.

I know you will understand that all correspondence and discussion of candidates must be absolutely confidential. If you consult other sources, please be sure that they also understand this. Premature consultation or publicity often causes the best qualified candidates to withdraw their names from consideration.

We thank you for your interest and help.

Sincerely yours,

Chairman
Presidential Search Committee

Enclosure (position description)

EXHIBIT K
Model Letter C:

To all nominated candidates who can be contacted directly.
Letter will be sent personal and confidential.

Date

Dear _____ :

_____ has nominated you as a candidate for President of X College. If you are interested in becoming an active candidate, please send us the following:

- an up-to-date *curriculum vita*.
- a statement outlining your interest in the position.
- a review of your strengths in relation to the position.
- the names, addresses and telephone numbers of three references.

Unless otherwise directed, we will keep all information regarding your candidacy confidential.

We have enclosed a Statement of Criteria for the President of X College as well as other information which should help in your response.

Thank you very much.

Sincerely yours,

Chairman
Presidential Search Committee

Enclosures (position description and general information)

EXHIBIT L
Model Letter D:

Less promising self-initiated applicants.
Letter will be sent personal and confidential.

Date

Dear _____ :

Thank you for your letter and supporting materials regarding your interest in the position of president of X College. I will forward your materials to the search committee which is now evaluating candidates. The committee does not expect to reach a decision until after the first of the year.

Unless otherwise directed, we will keep all information regarding your application confidential. All candidates will be notified of the final decision.

Thank you very much for your interest.

Sincerely yours,

Associate Dean of the College and
Coordinator of the Presidential Search

EXHIBIT M
Model Letter E:

To promising self-initiated candidates.
Letter sent personal and confidential.

Date

Dear _____ :

Thank you very much for your interest in the position of President of X College.

Enclosed for your consideration is a description of the position and some information about the college. If after reviewing these materials you continue to be interested in the presidency, please submit any additional information which you feel might be helpful to the committee including names, addresses and phone numbers of references who might provide useful information to support your candidacy.

Unless otherwise directed, we will keep all information regarding your application confidential. All candidates will be notified of the final decision.

Thank you very much.

Sincerely yours,

Chairman
Presidential Search Committee

Enclosures (Position description and general information)

EXHIBIT N
Sample of Interviewing Technique

Excerpts from the final report of the chairperson of a liberal arts college committee:

The committee was quite divided on the effectiveness of our interview procedures. The candidate would be allowed between one hour and one and one-half hours to talk to the committee. Generally, a subcommittee of five or six people would travel to New York, Chicago, or Los Angeles for interviews. . . . The committee developed a stock line of about seven questions, e.g.:

1. What is the future of the small, independent liberal arts college?
2. What is its purpose?
3. Can the self-imposed pressure on students be corrected?
4. How can the applicant pool be increased?
5. How do you view raising money for the college?

The candidates' answers and overall impression would then be rated and characteristics such as energy, humor, presence, intelligence, verbosity, warmth, leadership, and others were rated on an alphabetical system. The marking was tough and I believe the highest candidate received an A-. . . . It was recommended wisely that there be more of an overlap with committee members in their travels so that the rating system could be more uniform. It was also suggested that the committee have a specific rating sheet for each candidate.

I find it difficult to systematize such a subjective process. I think the candidates were by and large put at ease and given a chance to express their opinions on some very complex issues. Overall ratings were really quite consistent within the committee although there were often very real differences of opinion on a given characteristic. This entire procedure was designed to reduce the candidates from 30 down to five.

EXHIBIT O
Sample of Interviewing Technique

Concluding section of an elaborate interviewing process recently used by a midwestern institution suggesting ways of testing a candidate's breadth of view and intellectual agility.

Getting what you ask for, or being artistic about it.

Any candidate worth his/her salt is going to be sophisticated and sensitive to the rhetoric required. We can use this and/or try to sidestep it.

1. Use it—While we should seek very specific information, some general ritualistic questions ("the nature of liberal arts education", etc.) should be asked—more to give the candidate an opportunity to "shine" than to elicit "content." That is, we should throw candidates a few "high hard ones" to see if they can hit them out of the park.

2. Sidestep it—For what they are worth, here are a few time-honored ways of trying to get less "processed" news.

    a. Present both sides of a controversial issue as evenhandedly as possible.

      Sample: Some people have argued that the most important achievements of a liberal arts education must, by their nature, remain intangible and that insistence on so-called "objective" measurement is likely to result in their trivialization, their misrepresentation, or both.

                Other people have said that educators who are spending other people's money must be willing to be held accountable for their claims and are, therefore, morally responsible to nominate observable criteria against which outcomes may be evaluated. How do you feel about this?

    b. Ask wide open ("projective") questions: the assumption is that if nothing else, you will get whatever is most important/salient to the person. (Well, maybe.)

      Sample: If you could start from scratch and create the ideal college—the college of your dreams—what would it be like?
                Of all the things you have done as _____ , what has given you the most satisfaction?

    c. Ask questions which do not seem to have any "good" answer.

      Sample: What kind of college do you find the most difficult with which to work?

                If there were one thing in your professional life that you could do over differently, what would it be?

Looking at the requirements of this position, which do you think will come the most easily to you? Which will be the toughest?

d. Ask "provocative" or emotionally-loaded questions.

Sample: A number of academic institutions have felt that it was worthwhile to refuse government money in order to safeguard their autonomy. How do you feel about this?

It has been suggested that college enrollments follow pretty closely the financial payoffs of a college degree. If this is really why people go to college, wouldn't it be more honest to stop talking about the liberating effects of education and make sure that people's investment really pays off?

e. Be sure your question has been answered. Don't be afraid to restate or pursue something that has been evaded.

EXHIBIT P
Sample Letter to Candidates
Who are No Longer Being Considered

Dear _____ :

On behalf of the Presidential Search Committee I want to report on the status of your candidacy for the presidency of _____ . As I am sure you will appreciate, the task of selecting a small group of candidates whose qualifications appear to be the most relevant to to the current needs of _____ is most difficult. However, after our Committee's careful review of your resume, I regret to inform you that you are not among those individuals who are still being considered by our Committee.

We are most grateful for your willingness to let us review your resume. Thank you for your interest in _____—and best wishes in your future professional activities.

Sincerely,

Chairman
Presidential Search Committee

EXHIBIT Q
Campus Visit of Presidential Candidate

(From a discussion of Denison University's search process in the *Denison Alumnus*, cited previously.)

Sunday
4:30	Visit to Doane Library
6:30	Cocktails with 20 faculty members and spouses at the home of the Dean of College
8:00	Dinner at the home of the University Professor with four other faculty members.

Monday
8:00	Breakfast meeting with Provost
9:45	Meet with Vice President for Finance and Management
11:00	Meet with small group of faculty (9) to discuss curriculum
12:00	Informal luncheon in Student Union with faculty
1:15	Meet with Dean of Students
2:00	Tour of campus to include a visit to Burke Hall of music and art
3:15	Meet with faculty departmental representatives (30 people)
6:30	Cocktails and dinner at President's home (7 trustees, 9 others, and spouses)
10:30	Retire, Middleton House

Tuesday
8:00	Breakfast meeting with Director of University Relations (Development)
9:10	Meet with Dean of Admissions
10:00	Meet with small group of faculty (10) to discuss scholarship and research
11:00	Meet with small group of students (10)
12:00	Luncheon with alumni leaders
2:00	Meet with student representatives (22)
4:45	Depart Middleton House for Columbus Airport

EXHIBIT R
Sample Materials Provided Candidates

Bucknell University

1. *The Rise of Bucknell University*, J. Orin Oliphant
2. Charter of the University
3. Bylaws of Board of Trustees
4. University Catalog
5. Faculty Handbook
6. Administrative Handbook
7. Treasurer's Report (past 10 years)
8. Self-Study for Middle States Evaluation (1972-73)
9. President's Report (past 10 years)

Yankton College

1. College Catalog
2. Audit Report
3. Current Budget
4. Last accreditation report of the College
5. Conservatory of Music evaluation
6. Fiscal giving record (3-year breakdown by category of donor)
7. Enrollment figures for last three years
8. Five-year plan
9. Sample of Admissions material
10. Faculty Bylaws
11. Tenure Policy
12. Yankton College Standard (as adopted by students)
13. Form to be used in evaluating the candidate
14. *Only by request*—the Bylaws of the College

It was also felt that information regarding the community could be be obtained from the Chamber of Commerce and sent with the above material.

EXHIBIT S
Notice of Presidential Selection

The search for a new president of Hampshire College has come to a successful conclusion. The Board of Trustees has chosen Adele Smith Simmons. She will assume office on July 1, 1977.

Dr. Simmons has been Dean of Student Affairs at Princeton University since 1972. A graduate of Radcliffe College with honors in 1963, she received her doctoral degree from Oxford University in 1969. She was an Assistant Professor in History at Tufts University from 1969 to 1972 and an Assistant Dean from 1969 to 1970. She became Dean of Jackson College at Tufts in 1970. She has been a member of the Harvard University Board of Overseers since 1972. The new president is married and has two children.

The Search Committee is very proud of and enthusiastically supports the selection of Dr. Simmons from among a number of highly qualified candidates. The entire College community is looking forward to working with her as president.

The Committee wants to extend a special thanks to you for your participation in the search process. We appreciate your involvement and your interest in Hampshire College.

Mrs. Samuel L. Rosenberry
Chairman Presidential Search Committee

EXHIBIT T

To: Members of the Carleton Community

March 28, 1977

The Presidential Search Committee recommended to the Board of Trustees on March 11 that Robert Edwards become Carleton's seventh president. The recommendation was approved by the Board and I am happy to tell you that Mr. Edwards has accepted the appointment.

Mr. Edwards was born in 1935, attended public schools in Middletown, Ohio, and graduated from Deerfield Academy in 1953. He graduated from Princeton University magna cum laude in 1957, having majored in English. He read law for two years at Corpus Christi College, Cambridge, and graduated from Harvard University Law School in 1961.

After two years in Africa and two years in the State Department, he joined the Ford Foundation staff in 1965. His first major assignment occurred in 1969 when he was made representative of the Foundation's Pakistan field office, serving there until 1972 through the Indo-Pakistan War. He was responsible for administration of programs in agriculture, population, university development and educational planning.

Mr. Edwards then returned to the Foundation's New York office and shortly became head of their Mid-East and Africa program, the post he now holds. This involved a professional staff in New York and overseas of about 40 persons, in addition to about 65 project specialists.

The Search Committee has found Bob Edwards to be extraordinarily able, with a fine intellect and warm personality. His lack of professional experience in academia is felt to be no disadvantage, for Carleton's issues and opportunities can be viewed in a fresh perspective. His considerable administrative experience, as well as a humane and wise approach to complex issues, can be attested to by your committee.

Bob and Ellen Edwards have two daughters, Eliza, aged 9, and Daphne, aged 8. An addition to the family is expected in May. Mrs. Edwards attended Wellesley College. The family will arrive on campus on or about September 1. Present commitments at the Ford Foundation prevent an earlier arrival at Carleton, but it is Mr. Edwards' intention to spend at least two weeks at Carleton during the summer months.

Sincerely,

Thomas M. Crosby,
Chairman
Board of Trustees.

EXHIBIT U
Transition Planning for the New President
(Memorandum of an Administrative Officer)

It is my sense that we must do everything possible to exploit the advantages of a new presidency and to overcome the factors which usually inhibit a smooth transition and the early ability to deal effectively and decisively with not only routine matters, but also with more significant problems. I, therefore, propose that you appoint, as soon as possible, a transition team to do the following:

1. Establish and maintain a close working relationship with the new president during the period from the acceptance of the offer until the opening of the college in September.

2. Prepare and provide for the new president basic information about the college generally and about specific questions and problems. Both the new president and the transition team should take initiative in identifying areas in which information should be provided.

3. Provide information about and work with the new president in learning about the basic procedures and processes with which the president must be involved. These would be, for example, personnel policies and procedures, reappointments, budget planning and decision-making, etc.

4. Prepare and provide analysis and recommendations regarding some of the college's central problems. These would probably include:

    a. Admissions
    b. The development of a stable, accountable structure for academic leadership
    c. Student attrition
    d. The creation of a clear and widely understood sense within the college of the institution's mission
    e. Fundraising
    f. Organizational relationships and roles

The transition team should also initiate with the new president plans for the use of the new president's time in generating general publicity about the college. If the college is to get the most public relations advantage possible from a new president, we must plan well before September for the kind of publicity the college wants to generate and the media coverage, speaking engagements, participation in conferences, etc., with which the president should be involved.